The Challenge of
The New Millennium

Other Titles From New Falcon Publications

Cosmic Trigger: The Final Secret of the Illuminati
Prometheus Rising
    By Robert Anton Wilson
Undoing Yourself With Energized Meditation
Secrets of Western Tantra
    By Christopher S. Hyatt, Ph.D.
Eight Lectures on Yoga
The Pathworkings of Aleister Crowley
    By Aleister Crowley
Neuropolitique
The Game of Life
    By Timothy Leary, Ph.D.
Zen Without Zen Masters
    By Camden Benares
Condensed Chaos: An Introduction to Chaos Magic
    By Phil Hine
The Complete Golden Dawn System of Magic
The Golden Dawn Tapes—Series I, II, and III
    By Israel Regardie
Buddhism and Jungian Psychology
    By J. Marvin Spiegelman, Ph.D.
Astrology & Consciousness
    By Rio Olesky
Metaskills: The Spiritual Art of Therapy
    By Amy Mindell, Ph.D.
The Mysteries Revealed
    By Andrew Schneider
Beyond Duality: The Art of Transcendence
    By Laurence Galian
Soul Magic: Understanding Your Journey
    By Katherine Torres, Ph.D.
Aversion to Honor: A Tale of Sexual Harassment Within the Federal Gov't
    By Thomas R. Burns, Ph.D.
Carl Sagan & Immanuel Velikovsky
    By Charles Ginenthal

And to get your free catalog of *all* of our titles, write to:
NEW FALCON PUBLICATIONS (Catalog Dept.)
1739 East Broadway Road, Suite 1-277
Tempe, Arizona 85282 U.S.A.
And visit our website at http://www.newfalcon.com

THE CHALLENGE OF THE NEW MILLENNIUM

Winning the Struggle With Ourselves

Jerral R. Hicks, Ed.D.

NEW FALCON PUBLICATIONS
TEMPE, ARIZONA, U.S.A.

Copyright © 1997 by Jerral Hicks, Ed.D.

All rights reserved. No part of this book, in part or in whole, may be reproduced, transmitted, or utilized, in any form or by any means, electronic or mechanical, including photocopying, recording, or by any information storage and retrieval system, without permission in writing from the publisher, except for brief quotations in critical articles, books and reviews.

International Standard Book Number: 1-56184-125-0
Library of Congress Catalog Card Number: 97-65815

First Edition 1997

Cover Art by Denise Cuttitta

The paper used in this publication meets the minimum requirements of the American National Standard for Permanence of Paper for Printed Library Materials Z39.48-1984

Address all inquiries to:
New Falcon Publications
1739 East Broadway Road Suite 1-277
Tempe, AZ 85282 U.S.A.
(or)
1209 South Casino Center
Las Vegas, NV 89104 U.S.A.

To the dedicated parents and teachers of "the Fifties"

Table of Contents

Preface   11

Chapter I: Our Prehistoric Heritage   13
  The Beast Within   14
    The Nature of Instincts   16
    The Example of Our Sex Drive   18
  Our Prehistoric Instincts   20
    Territorialism   20
    Aggression   23
    Competition   24
    Social Order   25
    Power (Control)   26
    Fairness   28
    Logic/Problem Solving   29
    Fight/Flight   29
    Hunting   30
    Routine   32
    Family   32
    Emotions   34
    Reproduction   35
    Campfire/Fireplace   36
    Spiritualism   36
    Aesthetic Expression   39
    Language   39
    Play   40
    Concluding Thoughts About Their Role   40
  Different Behavior Modes   42
  A More Basic Perspective   44

Chapter II: Taming Of The Beast   46
  The Human Difference   48
    The Role of Learning   48
    Coping With Our Prehistoric Heritage   49
  Creating Socially Compatible Individuals   51
    Responsible Agents   51
    Techniques for Transmitting Values & Morals   52
    The Onset of Training   53

Values, Morals & Priorities	55
What They Are	56
How They Differ	57
How They Are Related	58
The Importance of Morality	59
Our Paradoxical Behaviors	60
Stages of Moral Maturity	61
Determining One's Stage of Moral Development	64
Today's Challenge	65
Chapter III: A Changed America	67
America, Circa 1950s	69
Social Control	69
Daily Living	72
Public Schools	75
The Family	77
Business Practices & Ethics	81
Politics	84
The Dark Side of the Fifties	86
Qualities Lost or Clearly Diminished	88
Where To From Here?	93
Chapter IV: Toward Survival of the Family & Good Parenting	95
The Family	
Development of the Family	96
Tomorrow's Family Needs	97
Tomorrow's Challenge: Good Parenting	98
Today's Child	99
The Challenge to Today's Parents	101
Why We Decide to Be Parents	102
Learning to Parent	103
Parenting for Success	104
Basic Principles About Child Development & Parenting	105
How to Raise a Loser in Life	114
Chapter V: Schools For Tomorrow's Needs	117
Purposes of Our Schools	119
The Hidden Curriculum	120
A Brief Review of Values & Morals in Our Schools	123
A Strategy for Teaching Children Moral Values	126
How to Teach	127
What to Teach	129
An Expanded Role for Our Schools	132

Chapter VI: Toward More Responsible Government & A Socially-Compatible, Responsible Citizenry   134
    A Fundamental Change   136
    The Downside of Public Assistance Programs   139
    Where We Go From Here   143
       Political Reforms   145
       Entitlement Policies & Other Policies   155
    Directions for Responsible Change   158
       Funding for Law Enforcement   160
       Tax Reform   161
       Subsidies for Producers of Products That Serve No
          Constructive Purpose   165
       Unlicensed & Uninsured Drivers   166
       Eligibility for Medicare & Social Security Benefits   166
       Agricultural Subsidies   168
       Assistance to Families with Dependent Children   169
       Limitation of Childbearing of Those on Assistance   170
       Mandatory Parent Training   172
       Mandatory Work & Job Training For Those on Assistance   173
       Responsible Management of Assistance Programs   173
       Purchase/Use of Firearms by Minors   174
       Mandatory Background Check of Those Who Purchase
          Firearms   174
       Restriction of Smokers & Drinking Drivers   175
       Curfews for Adolescents   176
       School Dropouts   177
       Mandatory Saving for Old Age   177
       Tax-Supported College Education   178
       Assistance & Benefits for Illegal Aliens   180
       Citizenship for Newborns   181
       Concluding Thoughts   182

About the Author   184

Index   185

PREFACE

This book should not be considered recreational reading. Rather, it should be viewed as a serious examination of what we are as a species, how we have changed as a society during the 30 years past, and what might be done to make society and life more pleasant and worthwhile. It takes a hard look at some unpleasant realities, some brutal truths about human nature. It examines our *dark side*—those forces deep within that compel many of us to behave in a destructive manner. And as clearly illustrated on the network TV news today, the picture is often grim.

But there's more to the story here in America. The family and parenting aren't what they used to be. Neither are our schools, neighborhoods, and towns. Nearly one-third of all childbirths are illegitimate, and drug use is widespread and growing. Our sense of community has diminished. So has our sense of personal responsibility. And a growing fear of crime has reduced our freedoms as we seek to limit risks of being victimized—avoiding certain areas at certain times, and avoiding other areas altogether. Many are deeply concerned about our future as a society and worry that America may disintegrate.

What compels so many to behave violently? Is there no hope for the future?

Through the ages, societies have striven to "mold" or shape each new generation into socially-compatible, rational beings who are able to live, work, and play in reasonable harmony. Specific institutions have been charged with this task. Traditionally, the family, the spiritual institutions, the community-at-large, and, relatively recently, the schools have borne the responsibility of shaping each new member into a socially and culturally-compatible being. And in this matter, America has been no different. But as noted above, America has undergone fundamental changes in recent decades. I believe we now face the proverbial "fork in the road." We can continue on the present course or plan and implement fundamental changes in our direction as a society. Given the deterioration of many aspects of society since the "Fifties" and the threat that those changes pose, we have no choice.

This study of what we are and where we are going, then, must also include an examination of how societies normally "mold" each new generation into socially-compatible, rational beings. The roles of the family, school, and other institutions in this task are examined, and changes in these institutions since the 1950s are considered—including the consequences of those changes.

I have dedicated this work to the parents and teachers of "the Fifties." Not because it was a time of universal harmony and justice in our society—because it wasn't, especially for minorities. But because it was a time of greater civility, a time when today's illegal drugs were largely unknown to teenagers, a time when children went to school without fear of being shot by a classmate, and a time when they commonly grew up in stable homes. In many respects, it was a time better suited for growing up in America. But I make no claim that I write for others of my generation. I write only for myself.

It is my hope that this work will promote a better understanding of us as a species and focus attention on some of the challenges confronting America in the third millennium. I also hope that it will stir my readers to become politically active so that needed political reforms and other changes can be implemented.

Jerral R. Hicks, Ed.D.
March, 1997

Chapter I

Our Prehistoric Heritage

Society is but a thin veneer that masks the beast within.

The veneer clearly seems to have become rather tenuous in recent years. The news media bombard us daily with violent events. If it's not a drive-by shooting or the rape of an elderly woman living alone, it's a hostage situation, a bomb, a murder in a domestic dispute, or a shooting in a drug deal gone bad. If it's not at a roadside park along an interstate or in a public housing project, it's on a school campus or in a convenience store. Only the names and places seem to change. Two disturbing trends seem to have emerged: violent crimes are increasingly affecting a wider spectrum of society, and young people are committing more and more of them.

Reports of events abroad often are much the same. The end of the rather structured atmosphere of the Cold War has apparently given way to uncertainty and unleashed long-simmering ethnic hatreds, resulting in violent power struggles. Car bombs continue to explode, humanitarian efforts are often overwhelmed by those displaced by war, and genocide is sometimes the official policy of those in power. If it's not in Europe or the Middle East, it's in Africa, Asia, or South America. Again, only the names and places seem to change. Radical governments that are based on hate and are determined to acquire chemical, biological, and nuclear weapons so they can "cleanse" the world pose even greater potential destruction.

Why do we behave in such destructive, often violent, ways? Is humanity destined to drop into a dark abyss? Unfortunately, the history of humanity is not very encouraging; from the beginning, it is, to a considerable extent, a story of violent conflicts between individuals and between groups. Is it unrealistic to hope for a better tomorrow?

No, it is not unrealistic. We need look no further than ourselves. Billions around the world go about their daily lives, refusing to let their frustrations, anxieties, and occasional anti-social, sometimes violent, urges disrupt their goals, family life, and work. Instead of acting out anti-social urges, we keep our emotions in check and go about quite normal, socially compatible lives. This is also apparent in the affairs of nations. The orderly division of Czechoslovakia along ethnic lines into two separate states is a superb example of how we *can* behave toward one another and deal with problems in a sensible, non-violent manner. In Czechoslovakia, people brought about change through a democratic process based on respect and honor of the wishes of each citizen. As a matter of fact, many Czechs and Slovaks believe that the breakup along ethnic lines was unnecessary and hope for a reunion.

THE BEAST WITHIN

Hope for a better tomorrow rests first on an understanding of ourselves. This requires, among other things, an understanding of those innate forces that *predispose* us to behave in certain, sometimes destructive, ways. But as a thinking animal, aren't our behaviors determined by conscious thoughts and efforts to solve real problems encounter in everyday living? Aren't our futures determined by rational decisions, not by hazy, innate forces that predispose us to behave in particular ways? Yes, but only in part. Innate forces do predispose us to behave in certain ways. Taken as a group, they play a major role in defining what it means to be human—and reveal our similarities to many other animals. Under certain circumstances, they even burst to the surface to dominate our behaviors and cause us to do specific things. Freedom of choice, then, really isn't as free as it seems.

Although these forces may suddenly burst to the surface to dominate our behaviors in specific situations, such as a violent response to discovery of an unfaithful spouse, they often impact behaviors in a subtle, yet pervasive manner. And as automated behavioral tendencies, they don't require conscious thought to affect behavior. We just think and act in certain ways because they are a part of us. Many of our behaviors, then, are predictable and appear both as specific responses to specific situations and as common behavioral patterns without regard to family, community, or society.

How are these "forces" manifested in our behaviors? They play a major role in the turf wars between gangs, where we sit at the dinner table, the content of TV programs, church attendance, competitions of all kinds, thrill-seekers who flirt with death, TV commercials, wars between nations, the fireplace in our home, Halloween, and Christmas. Our love of the outdoors, popular sports, families, music, art, and other forms of expression are also impacted to some degree by these forces. Even our existence is a result of these forces. They are inescapable.

What are these forces? They are those prehistoric instincts within that manifest themselves in countless ways, including what is often referred to as "our dark side." And it is our "dark side," the anti-social, destructive impact of these instincts, that the media focuses on and which worries us today. We see them at work every day, whether in violent domestic disputes, angry confrontations between drivers on the freeway, battles for custody of children, drive-by shootings, or ethnic warfare. Judging from the network news, these forces seem to be playing a growing role in society—and in the world. Of course these instincts may, as noted above, also manifest themselves in non-violent, seemingly harmless behavioral patterns, such as our tendency to sit in a particular chair at the dinner table. But even these *can* lead to confrontations.

Whatever the case, more and more of us apparently are slipping through the proverbial "cracks" of society. Jails are overcrowded nationwide; we can't build enough. Increasing numbers of young people seem to display a cold, uncaring attitude toward others. We read about young people who have little regard for human life and commit senseless shootings, whether the victim is a German tourist in Florida or a convenience store clerk in Oregon. Every day we hear about people lying, cheating, stealing, and killing to get what they *value*. For them, what's *right* and what's *wrong* are just a matter of what they *want*. The destruction they impose on others is irrelevant.

Essentially, the role of society is to establish and maintain institutions and processes that "mold" each of us into beings who are able to live together in a harmonious fashion. This requires keeping our destructive, anti-social urges in check. But, as noted above, we increasingly seem to be falling short. Why? During the past two or three decades, some socializing institutions have either been discarded or now play a diminished role in society. When combined with the greater freedom to "do your own thing" and to "experience" life, management of the destructive side of our instincts has become increasingly difficult. We now see such a resurgence of *the beast within* that it threatens the basic fabric of society. Indeed, enforcement of legal controls has become a nightmare! If we are to cope with these forces adequately, we must first recognize and understand them. Then we can examine how societies normally keep them in check and consider what changes need to be implemented.

The Nature of Instincts

What exactly is an instinct? An instinct is an inborn tendency of members of a species to behave in a particular manner. It originates as part of a specie's overall struggle to meet those needs that are essential to its survival, such as securing food, avoiding threats from predators, and reproduction. It develops from trial-and-error efforts to satisfy a specific need which, eventually, lead to the discovery of the behavior that most efficiently satisfies that need. Incidental repetition leads to this discovery which, in turn, leads to the development of a behavioral pattern that is eventually encoded in the brain of the species and becomes part of the genetic code that is passed on from one generation to the next. And since those members of a species that practice the most effective behaviors are the most likely to survive, their instincts are most likely to be passed on to future generations.

Instincts, then, are natural consequences in animal life and are inherently "good" in the environment in which they develop because they enhance a specie's chances of survival. They should not be construed as "demonic" or evil—as is sometimes the case in religious cults and even in some mainline religions. There is nothing sinister or "devilish" in their origin. They are just natural consequences in animal life on our planet. As in other species, then, instincts are a natural part of us.

Some instincts are environment-specific, while others are so basic that they develop without regard to environmental variations. For example, some animals became nocturnal feeders because it was easier to catch preferred prey at night. Others became nocturnal to avoid extreme daytime temperatures. These are environment-specific instincts. That is, they are specific adaptations to specific environmental conditions. Others, such as *territorialism* and *reproduction,* are so basic that they appear in virtually all species and in all environments.

Instinctual behaviors may be triggered by internal factors or by environmental stimuli. For example, the longer, warming days of late spring signal the American elk to migrate to higher elevations where grass becomes plentiful, but shorter days and cooling temperatures in the fall signal a retreat to lower elevations to escape harsh winter conditions and where food supplies are more accessible. In contrast, the mating in many other species is normally triggered by hormonal changes within the female. (Of course, this internal factor is influenced in some species by environmental factors since they tend to reproduce during a given season of the year.) Whatever the case, these behaviors appear spontaneously, without forethought. The appearance of some instinctual behaviors, then, is determined by internal or developmental factors, while others are triggered by environmental circumstances.

Instincts are entirely appropriate for the environment in which they develop. Otherwise, they would not develop. Those that developed in our early, prehistoric ancestors, then, were quite appropriate for a violent world where there were frequent threats from predators, and where the threat of starvation drove them in a competitive search for food. Whatever social structure that existed in that environment was simpler than is common in today's modern, complex societies where individuals are highly dependent on each other. Survival was largely an individual matter. Those who were stronger and quicker were more likely to escape from predators, and, when they began forming groups, they were better able to dominate others of their kind. Typically, those who were more aggressive got a bigger share of food, got more mates, and so on. Those who were smarter were able to outwit and catch more prey. Disputes between members of a species were normally settled by intimidation or brute force. It was a world ruled by the strongest, quickest, smartest, and most aggressive. (This is still the rule in most animals.) Compassion and thoughtful respect of each other's needs didn't exist. Neither did individual rights, entitlements, morals, and fairness.

Instincts also have an enduring quality. Once developed, they are resistant to change, often continuing into distant future generations where their usefulness no longer exists or is problematic. (This tends to limit a species' ability to adapt to changes in the environment, and has probably contributed to the demise of some species, such as the disappearance of Neanderthal man. Today's rapid changes in the interior of Brazil present a similar threat to the existence of many species, including the native human inhabitants.) This quality has significant implications: Instincts within us today have their origins in the distant, prehistoric environment described above. The problem today is, some instincts that were necessary for survival in a primitive, often violent environment are incompatible with behavioral expectations in today's modern societies. Today we are highly interdependent, and we are expected to be considerate of each other's "rights" and to settle differences in nonviolent ways. And herein lies the challenge that confronts societies around the world today: how to cope with prehistoric instincts that are basically incompatible in today's world.

The Example of Our Sex Drive

Behaviors related to our sex drive provide countless examples of the sometimes destructive power of instincts. Otherwise, there would be no unwanted pregnancies, no sexually-transmitted diseases, no incest, and no families destroyed by infidelity. There would be no sexual abuse of children, and rape would not exist. We would always do the rational thing. But we don't. Sexual abuse of children and the probability that one out of every four women in America will be a victim of rape or attempted rape during her lifetime are sad testimonials to the difficulty of controlling this ancient instinct. Revelations that priests and other members of the clergy have had sexual relationships with parishioners and have sexually abused youngsters in their trust also verify the power of the sex drive and underscore the difficulty of channeling this instinct in socially acceptable ways. Decisions apparently based solely on the need for immediate sexual gratification, then, complicate the lives of many of us and make it more difficult to achieve goals, sometimes even erase goals. The futures of many are greatly affected by the consequences of passionate actions during adolescence or early adulthood. Unwanted pregnancies make completion of high school and college educations more difficult, AIDS is spreading at an alarming rate, even though we know how to avoid contracting it, and many married people risk their marriages by having extra-marital relationships. Let's face it—we are nearly always first "attracted" to each other because of physical appearance or sex appeal. Whoever heard of men seeking extramarital affairs because they were looking for better cooks? And women who attracted men because they were efficient co-workers or neat housekeepers?

As in other species, the sex drive provides the means of continuing our existence. But, unbridled, it is one of the basic components of *the beast within.* Controlling this beast, then, has been one of the primary challenges confronting countless societies through the ages.

To understand better the role that this ancient instinct plays in our species, we first need to examine the role of the sex drive as commonly found in most animals. As one of the three basic forces in the lives of animals—the need for food, shelter/protection from threats, and reproduction, the reproductive instinct plays a major role. More specifically, for most animals, copulation is merely a response to the reproductive instinct, a matter of survival of the species. It occurs infrequently, and only when the female is "in season." This period is determined by the female's ovulation which is accompanied by and communicated to the male through scents (perfumes?) and ritualized behaviors (flirting?). Sound familiar? Detection of the female's scent by the male triggers a ritualized pursuit, culminating in copulation. After copulation, the female and male usually go their separate ways. Prior to birth, the *nesting instinct* triggers preparation of a place for giving birth or laying eggs. Upon giving birth, the maternal instinct triggers cuddling, feeding and other nurturing behaviors. In some species, the male responds to a paternal instinct and assists in parenting duties. But in many species, raising the young is solely the task of the mother.

While copulation is an infrequent physiological event in most animals, we are, to say the least, somewhat different. Following puberty, the sex drive plays a major role in our thoughts and various overt behaviors. Sexual fantasies, wet dreams, and masturbation become very common, and individuals pursue relationships with others that often lead to sexual intimacy. Although "one night stands" or "hit-and-runs" do occur, most of us eventually pair off with someone whom we find "attractive" and establish an ongoing relationship. (A long-term relationship is advantageous because our young, who are totally helpless at birth, mature relatively slowly and require considerable protection and nurturing during the process.) And, inevitably, copulation plays a significant role in the maintenance of this "mature" relationship of a couple. It is not merely a physiological response to an instinct that produces offspring; it is also an emotional and social experience—one that plays an important part in the bonding of a couple. Copulation, then, doesn't occur only during the brief period of fertility each month; it may occur whenever the physical need or need for emotional reassurance necessitates. Receptiveness may be signaled in a variety of ways, such as a certain type of eye contact, a manner of walking, or even one's presence, for example, at a party, dance, or single's bar. (Of course, they all aren't "single," and nowadays there is another meaning for "party.") Whole industries, such as cosmetics, are based on this desire to be "attractive" and "find someone." This is underlined by sales of "fragrances" (scents) and other cosmetics that run into the billions of dollars each year just in the United States. Appeal to the sex drive is also apparent in the design of clothing and cars, in the lyrics of music, in movies, in popular sports, and especially in advertising. Movie stars act out love scenes, singers wail over lost love, and models provocatively display the latest jeans. As a matter of fact, the lyrics of most popular songs focus on the search for love, the joy of love, love lost, and coping with problems in love relationships. We seem preoccupied with sex. We discuss oral sex (and other formerly unmentionables) on TV talk shows, advertise condoms on TV, tell countless dirty jokes, buy romance novels by the millions, and spend billions on music videos and movies that include explicit references to sex or sex scenes. Like the lyrics of a popular song, it seems that we "just can't get enough."

The sex drive does indeed play an important role in our lives. It is even the focus of many of our daily fantasies. Just think how often we mentally undress those we find sexually attractive. With the total human population rapidly approaching six billion, we obviously "do it" much more often than is necessary to ensure survival of our species. "Romance" apparently is a source of considerable enjoyment and a powerful force in life.

OUR PREHISTORIC INSTINCTS

What instincts are apparent in our species? While a comprehensive description of all of our instincts isn't necessary here, inclusion of those below is useful. Some play a more obvious, important role; others are less important but are included because they help illustrate the impact of instincts in our lives. It could be argued that some are cultural phenomena. But whatever the case, they are included because they appear or develop spontaneously in group-living environments and are common to virtually all human societies. Many are also found in other animal species.

Territorialism

Territorialism is our tendency to become emotionally attached to and possessive of our surroundings, including places, things, other individuals, even our jobs, ideas, and reputations—whatever we regard as "ours" or "mine." It is one of the most powerful and most visible instincts. It developed as a result of our earliest ancestors' competition for hunting and "nesting" space. A familiar environment not only enhanced their chances of survival, it also was reassuring in a world full of threats.

Beginning at an early age, *territorialism* plays a very pervasive role in life. It is the source of conflicts between young children who fight over what is "mine," and it accounts for our discomfort when someone sits in "my" chair at the dinner table. It is the source of conflicts between gangs who fight over "turf," companies that battle over market share, drivers who angrily contend for their lane on the freeway, and nations that battle over land, water rights, and other resources. *Territorialism* is also the driving force in love triangles and broken marriages that end in violence. ("If I can't have you, nobody can! You're not getting my money! I'm getting custody of my kids!") Today's manifestations of this instinct, then, are usually thought of as property and property rights.

Personal ownership of property requires that we communicate our individual claims to each other. Of course we are not alone in this matter. Members of most other species "mark" their territory as a means of communicating their individual claims to others of their kind. This is accomplished through various sounds, scents, and body language. Bull elk bugle, birds sing, bears claw trees, and dogs and cats leave scents. But instead of marking our territory with claw marks or scents, we mark it with fences, matching wedding bands, flags, and all sorts of printed signs, which range from graffiti and *No Trespassing* signs, to labels, license plates, brands on livestock, and copyright notices. Couples walk together hand-in-hand, sharing each other's personal space, and we carry pictures of loved ones in our wallets. All these announce that something or someone is "mine." But as in other species, signs are sometimes disregarded, claims are challenged, and we are compelled to defend our territory. So we get into heated arguments, lawsuits, fist fights, and wars. As a matter of fact, the legal profession and laws exist to a large extent because of disputes related to this instinct, which range from child custody rights and division of various properties in divorces, to copyright and patent infringements, failure to fulfill contracts, property damages, theft, and violent acts that spring from property conflicts.

Territorialism, or more specifically, property ownership, normally plays a significant role in community status and in our relationships with one another. We regularly judge each other and establish associations with each other, in part, according to how much we *have*. (Image *is* important.) For some, it is even a factor in their selection of a marriage partner. Territorialism is the origin of the dowry, and, in those societies where the dowry remains a custom, it is often *the* determining factor in selection of a marriage partner.

Territorialism even plays a major role in our identity as individuals. We commonly refer to our possessions as we do our body parts: *my* car, *my* job, *my* house, *my* wife, *my* (college) degree, and so on.

(This instinct is also signaled with other possessive pronouns and countless possessive nouns.) In a very real sense, then, our possessions are a part of us. This explains our nostalgia for old times, places, and things, and why we often feel an emotional loss when we part with a car or other possession that has served us well. Likewise, territorialism is usually the basis for a parent's tears at a son's or daughter's wedding, and the reason for tears at a funeral. Both events mark a "personal loss" of someone who was *ours*. It also explains why a house doesn't feel like home until our "personal things" are put in place and it becomes a part of us. Possessions, then, help give meaning to life and help us establish our identity as individuals.

As new possessions are acquired and old ones lost, our identity changes. We get a college degree and become an accountant or a teacher; a loved one dies and we search for a new meaning of life; and we have a child and become a parent. We get our driver's license and become a driver; we lose our job and become an unemployed person. These all affect how we see ourselves, our feelings of self-worth and self-confidence. This also explains the often greater self-confidence and assertiveness in those who experience a major property gain—such as a winner of a big lottery, or someone who marries into a wealthy family. Some even develop an air of importance, and become outspoken and condescending toward others. But new wealth doesn't result just in a new identity. It also may change one's social status—which includes new social activities and new friends. Old friends may be discarded.

On the other hand, as clearly illustrated in the suicides following the stock market crash of 1929, a major property loss can have a devastating impact on our identity and feeling of self-worth. It also explains why some react violently toward others when they are fired from *their* job, when a spouse files for a divorce, or when a major business deal goes bad. Such a property loss is an unacceptable threat to their self-esteem and their identity—even their survival. Lacking sufficient self-constraints, forces of *the beast within*—rage, revenge, and hatred, compel them to strike back.

Compounding the potential problems associated with *territorialism* is the tendency to want *more,* whether it is land, cash savings, a bigger house, or a greater share of a market. The statement in the advertisement, "You can't be too rich," appeals to this common desire. Territorialism, then, continues to play a major role in our personal lives, in world events, and in virtually all societies.

Aggression

This behavioral trait is intertwined with the *power* instinct and the *competition* instinct. As our ancient ancestors competed for the control of resources, mates, and status, they characteristically resorted to physical *aggression* when intimidation failed. As they became more sophisticated, they began bargaining to get what they wanted, but continued to resort to intimidation and physical *aggression* when necessary. The winner, the one who got his choice of mate, who ate his share of the kill first, who got to lead the pack, often was the one who was the most brutal. Examples abound today, from gang leaders to leaders of some nations.

This instinct wields considerable power today. It can even drive us to kill "enemies." And unlike the shark, which some have proclaimed to be "the perfect killing machine," we don't just kill for food. We kill our own for an endless number of reasons. We kill for revenge, for material gain, out of rage, as a matter of patriotic duty, out of jealousy, for political gain (power), to punish wrongdoers, to "cleanse" the world of evil, even as a result of hatred as revealed in, "I hate gays/blacks/ whites/Jews/women/Catholics.... The list is endless. Some kill for little apparent reason at all: "I didn't like the way he looked at me." Even job disputes and ongoing disputes between neighbors sometimes end in fatal shootings. The ugly truth is, most of us have, at some point, felt the *urge* to kill. Many have even fantasized killing someone. We just don't act it out because the likely consequences of doing so make it unattractive.

Every day there are countless examples that illustrate the role that *aggression* plays in life. They range from a wide variety of aggressive acts against individuals—such as domestic violence—to "ethnic cleansing" among ethnic groups, and warfare among nations. Various forms of "entertainment" that allow us to satisfy this instinct vicariously provide more examples. Otherwise, football, soccer, the Indy 500, boxing, bullfighting, and other aggressive spectator sports wouldn't exist, TV programs wouldn't include hundreds of violent acts each week, and school children wouldn't quickly gather to watch classmates fight. And this brings us to another ugly point about human nature: There is a part of us that is *drawn* to aggressive violence. Just as our ancestors were compelled to watch the feeding of the lions in the Roman Coliseum and hangings of horse thieves on the frontier, a part of us *needs* to watch violently aggressive acts. And the more violent they are, the more we are drawn to them. The most anticipated event at the rodeo is bull riding, the high point of a boxing match is a bloody knockout punch, and the most compelling subject in countless films about marine life is the vicious attack of the shark.

Societies commonly reinforce this instinct by rewarding the most aggressive. Superbowl winners get more than the losers, boxing champions get bigger purses, and aggressive salespeople get bigger bonuses. The familiar expression, "The squeaky wheel gets the grease," is based on this common practice.

Competition

This instinct was a key element in Darwin's "survival of the fittest." He asserted that animals had competed for food and other limited resources from the beginning. The one who got there first got the most—and was most likely to survive. We see this at work today in movies about African wildlife. Today the desire to be "number one," whether in baseball or in sales, clearly indicates that this instinct also is alive and well in us. We also see it in our children when they rush, push, and shove to be first in line—even where there is no material reward for being first. Even our basic economic system, capitalism, is designed in large part around this instinct. Capitalism includes incentives for the individual who competes aggressively in his business operations: He is rewarded financially and allowed to accumulate his own property or "wealth." Provision for *competition* and *territorialism* in our capitalistic system has provided a key advantage over other economic systems. Indeed, lack of provision for these instincts on the individual level doomed communism from the beginning. *Competition* is a driving force in athletic contests, art shows, beauty pageants, competition among TV talk shows to be "Number One," and countless other "competitions" in societies around the world. It plays a key role, then, in many facets of human behavior—from success or failure in the corporate world, to feelings of ecstasy and indescribable loss in junior high school cheerleader competitions.

Like most other instincts, *competition* may have destructive or constructive consequences. For example, President John F. Kennedy galvanized support for his plan to land a man on the moon when he portrayed it as a race with the Soviet Union. We *had* to beat them. But competition also contributes to corporate espionage, student cheating to beat others, and various health problems related to competition-induced stress. It even led to disputed claims in the search for the AIDS virus. But it also will likely contribute to a quicker discovery of a cure for AIDS.

Social Order

One of the more enduring qualities of animal life has been the tendency of members of most species to organize themselves into groups. Today these groups are variously referred to as troops, schools, prides, herds, flocks, and so on. Our early ancestors were no different. At some point, they, too, began organizing themselves into groups. (This probably progressed from the clan to the tribe or village, then the city, the nation, and, finally, groups of nations.) This grouping instinct originated out of necessity: Chances of survival were enhanced when members banded together. Grouping, however, necessitated the establishment of some type of social structure and rules governing how members would interact. Typically, a hierarchy or "pecking order" was established for feeding, breeding, and power sharing, and rules establishing what was and what was not acceptable behavior. The role and status of individual members were usually determined by the sex, physical strength, and age of each member. Among our ancient ancestors, *fairness* also became a determining factor as members bargained for position and various resources.

Today some degree of *social order* is essential in all societies. (Otherwise, there would be no societies—only chaos.) It is based on common understandings about *what is* and *what is not* appropriate behavior within the society. When a socio-political structure collapses, as in an armed revolution or the collapse of an economy, some degree of uncertainty or chaos reigns until a new order or structure is established.

In today's world, we organize ourselves for many of the same reasons that our ancient ancestors did: to satisfy emotional and social needs, to secure power (and protection), and for material gain. Teenagers form clubs, cliques, and gangs; college students join fraternities and sororities; people in business join the Rotary and the Lions; professionals and retirees form groups to promote and protect their interests; and millions join country clubs. Workers join unions for bargaining power, mothers band together against drunk drivers, those who hold similar philosophical beliefs form political parties, and nations form trading blocks and military alliances. There is just no end to organizations.

Power (Control)

Like many other species, when our early ancestors began forming groups, they began organizing themselves according to a pecking order or power structure. Someone became the leader, ultimately responsible for major decisions, and others became responsible for various role tasks. Typically, the more power one had, the more benefits he enjoyed. This continues to be the case in organizations, whether it is a club, a labor union, a university government, a corporate hierarchy, or a national government. It is not surprising, then, that individuals have competed for positions of power and the benefits associated with them since ancient times. Those in leadership (power) positions have struggled to control others through physical violence, intimidation, threats, and persuasion, including rewards. Some have even sought to maintain their power by demonstrating their control of spirits and natural elements, such as rain, through rituals and ceremonies.

Weapons are intertwined with this instinct. How so? Although the earliest weapons were most likely developed to enhance success rates when hunting, they became tools for gaining power when our ancestors realized that they could be equally effective against rival individuals within a group and against other clans and tribes with whom they competed for hunting territory and other resources. Weapons, then, became instruments of *power*—a means of acquiring control over others.

Today the shift in emphasis from developing weapons for hunting to development of weapons for killing "enemies" is most apparent in weapons programs of nations. As a matter of fact, weapons developed by today's nations are developed exclusively for killing people—not hunting. These weapons, beginning with the simple throwing of stones by our primitive ancestors and progressing to today's MIRVED nuclear warheads on intercontinental missiles, have become increasingly complex and destructive. So we have the machine gun, the M1A1 tank, biological weapons, the AK-47, the F-15, and the aircraft carrier—weapons which are quite inappropriate for killing a deer. Of course we still provide those for the private sector, including the "Saturday night special."

Huge amounts of resources continue to be allotted to the research and development of weapons. (Dare we not continue in today's world?) Even *Third World* nations scramble to acquire the greatest instrument of power—"the bomb." The formation of nation-states

The Challenge of the New Millennium

centuries ago helped bring this about by bringing resources together on a scale previously unknown. This gathering of resources, especially brain power, also accelerated the pace of weapons development. It resulted, for example, in the race for "the bomb" during World War II. More recently, the advantage of being ahead technologically was vividly illustrated with our high-tech weapons in Desert Storm. We cheered at the deadly accuracy of our latest high-tech weapons and took pride in how quickly and how completely our laser-guided bombs, cruise missiles, A-10s, Apache helicopters, and M1A1 tanks overwhelmed opposing Iraqi forces.

The desire for *power* is also apparent in our fantasies. Just think how often we fantasize that we occupy positions of power or importance that people look up to. Some of us, for example, often sing along with a song and imagine ourselves on stage as we drive down the road.

The desire for *power* is also a factor when those in power positions, such as popular singers, successful businessmen, and political leaders, are pursued by those who wish to have a firsthand relationship with them—if nothing else, a "one night stand." This occurs because of one of the underlying principles in human relationships: When someone establishes a relationship as an equal with another in one respect, he psychologically tends to assume the status as an equal in other respects. This explains why the secretary, who is having an affair with a vice-president, becomes more confident, develops an "air of importance," and gets "pushy" with other secretaries. She assumes the status and power of her lover. It also explains why many eagerly gather around political leaders to serve and work for them; in doing so, they become part of a power elite and commonly enjoy some of the benefits bestowed on their leader. And, of course, their leader dispenses benefits to them—his "worker bees." Fans who pursue personal relationships with professional athletes and others of celebrity status do so for much the same reason. Such associations allow them to assume a new level (real or imagined) of notoriety and status. As they gain notoriety and status, their perceived power is increased.

Unfortunately, even spiritual leaders sometimes resort to primitive, violent forces to retain or expand their *power*—under the guise of the destruction of evil. Centuries ago, the Crusaders fought to regain control of the Holy Land. In Iran during the 1970s, a religious leader gained control of a government and society by inspiring his followers to violent revolution; forces of hate and revenge were unleashed to rid the country of "satanic" Western influences. The violence continues. In America, religious zealots have killed personnel at abortion clinics; others have carried out deadly suicide missions. For them, and for those who follow, the end (control or power) justifies the means. The lessons of Mandela and Tutu in South Africa, Mahatma Gandhi in India, and Martin Luther King, Jr. in America, go unlearned.

Fairness

At some point after they began forming groups, our distant ancestors decided that there had to be a better way of settling conflicts than by physical aggression. This likely started when groups or individuals of roughly equal strength (and threat to each other) realized that it was better to get a part of something without risk of injury or death than it was to risk injury or death and possibly get nothing. They eventually began negotiating how the "kill" would be divided, who would be responsible for which daily task, when to move on to another campsite, and rules governing social interactions among clan, then tribe members. As they hammered out agreements over the millennia, their bargaining enabled them to develop a keen sense of *fairness*. Today, deciding what is right or fair is the purpose of the judiciary, and it is the basis of social and business agreements of all kinds between individuals, corporations, and nations.

Children begin developing a sense of fairness at an early age—just listen to them bargain, "I'll let you...if you'll..." and "I'll trade you my...for your..." As they bargain they develop and refine their concept of *fairness*. And, as in adults, it becomes a rather pervasive concept in their thinking. Just listen to them complain to their parents, teachers, or peers, "That's not fair." This sense of *fairness*, then, is instinctual in nature because it is a key factor in human interactions and it begins to develop at an early age.

It is also a powerful force. Standards about *fairness* are the basis of court decisions; they affect the nature of agreements, how friends interact, and how spouses treat each other. Mutually beneficial relationships between individuals, between groups, and between nations are based on a sense of mutual trust that grows from being treated fairly. On the other hand, couples divorce, partnerships dissolve, and nations go to war when one party violates the others belief about what is fair and destroys the trust that is essential to the relationship.

Logic/Problem Solving

When confronted with threats or obstacles, we automatically try to "figure out" a way of dealing with them. This requires an awareness of a goal, the ability to analyze the nature of any threat or obstruction, formulation of a plan for eliminating or circumventing the threat, implementation of the plan, and the ability to make adjustments during the process as needed. Development of this ability to examine and solve problems began with our primitive predecessors' ongoing challenge to survive, whether it was finding food, avoiding being eaten, searching for water, or protecting themselves from weather. This, of course, also led to the development of weapons as they sought an advantage over other animals, the wearing of furs for protection from the cold, and countless other inventions through the millennia. And, like the recurve hunting bow, new inventions often incorporated the technology of earlier related developments—technology became increasingly complex. Development of *logic* and *problem solving abilities,* then, was inevitable: As our primitive predecessors exercised their limited mental faculties in their struggle to survive, their intellect expanded.

Fight/Flight

When our primitive ancestors were threatened by critters that attempted to eat them or rob them of food, they either had to fight or flee. Those who exhibited enhanced physical abilities when threatened were more likely to survive. Eventually, this characteristic was encoded into their genetic makeup as the fight/flight instinct. How did this instinct increase their chances of survival? When threatened, the fight/flight instinct triggered a sudden production of adrenaline and other stress hormones which, in turn, caused a variety of physiological changes, such as a more rapid heartbeat and increased muscle tension. These changes enhanced their abilities to fight and run.

But the *fight/flight* instinct isn't triggered just by physical threats. Disparaging remarks about one's personal integrity or family life also may be interpreted as threats and trigger this instinct. This explains why some individuals react angrily when they are called what they consider to be a derogatory name. In such situations, the threat to their character produces an adrenaline rush that, in turn, triggers strong emotions. And they either fight or flee. In today's modern societies, the fight response may be in the form of a physical attack, a heated argument, or a lawsuit.

The rush of adrenaline that accompanies a perceived threat produces an emotional "high" of sorts. This explains why modern societies have institutionalized popular spectator sports, such as boxing, hockey, and bullfighting, and other forms of "entertainment," such as action-adventure and horror movies, video games, and Halloween. They serve as outlets for this instinct by allowing individuals to feel the rush of adrenaline through vicarious experiences. Cheerleaders promote this in "fight, fight, fight, win, win, win" chants. Unfortunately, crowds at some of these events occasionally get out of hand when their adrenaline level and accompanying excitement cause them to act out emotions when the game doesn't turn out the way they like. This adrenaline rush even accounts, in part, for the lure of horse racing, slot machines, and other forms of gambling. Crowds yell and pound on the railing as the horses pound down the track. It's no wonder that gambling, football, and video games become addictive. The adrenaline "high" is irresistible.

The lure of this instinct is also apparent in *danger and escape games* such as riding roller coasters, sky diving, and bungee jumping. We enjoy these games because they present a very real risk which, in turn, creates fear and an adrenaline rush. Those who can accept the level of fear inherent in such games do so because the adrenaline rush is irresistible. Like children who enjoy horror movies, we *like* being scared because it feels good.

Hunting

Meat was an important part of our primitive ancestors' diet. Later ancestors learned to use furs from prey to protect them from the elements, use bones as tools, and use strips of hide to fasten things together. How did they obtain the needed meat, bones, hides, and furs? Like other predators, hunting. Survival, then, depended heavily on hunting skills.

Hunting also played a dominant role in our early ancestors' cultural development because it required them to be nomadic as they searched for prey. (Sometime later, some groups developed a sedentary lifestyle as they began eating and growing various plants.) Rituals and ceremonies soliciting the assistance of spirits in hunts and expressing gratitude to spirits for successful hunts became common. Hunting also became a major theme in their art. As a matter of fact, ancient artwork remaining on cave walls and rocks commonly depicts desired prey and hunting scenes. Hunting continues to play

The Challenge of the New Millennium

an important role in the lives of some indigenous groups deep in the Amazon Basin and other remote areas.

Today, hundreds of thousands of us hunt, not as a matter of survival, but as a matter of recreation. All sorts of "game animals" are hunted, from rabbits and alligators to ducks and bears. We enjoy the challenge of matching wits with prey and the excitement (adrenaline surge) of the kill. Some get so excited at the moment of the kill that they tremble with excitement or, as deer hunters call it, "get the buckachers." (I remember one hunter's retort when teased about his buckachers: "When I quit gettin' the buckachers, I'll quit huntin'.") Some hunt because it allows them to "get back to nature," to escape the pressures of modern living. The lure of the quiet, still morning and first stirrings of animals is irresistible—just as are the evenings.

Unfortunately, this instinct is also apparent today in the destructive, predatorial behaviors of those who victimize others. Stalkers and other types of predators hunt for victims at preferred places, such as rest areas along interstate highways, in shopping mall parking lots, and at airports. Gang members hunt for intruders from opposing gangs as they patrol their turf, and occasionally raid each other's territory, hunting and attacking "enemies" to demonstrate their superiority. Initiation into gangs sometimes even requires new members to seek out and commit violent acts against specific targets. These behaviors are examples of the hunting instinct in its most socially destructive, primitive form. Other predators, such as panhandlers and pickpockets, present less of a threat to the victim's physical well-being, but hunt for victims, nevertheless, as they size up a crowd looking for the most vulnerable, then make their "move." Still others use a more sophisticated approach. Instead of physically attacking their victim, they first gain his confidence as part of a "scam", then take advantage. Those who seek out the elderly or others to defraud them of their savings are examples of this type of hunter. Although they present little threat to the victim's physical well-being, they are also destructive, anti-social manifestations of this instinct.

Then there's the social hunter, the individual who is hunting for a relationship with someone for purely social reasons—which range from "one night stands" to long-term relationships. These hunters are commonly found in single's bars, at parties, on the ski slope, on school and college campuses, and, more recently, in grocery stores. As a matter of fact, someone who is "looking (hunting) for someone" can be anywhere. We all normally do this at some point in our lives.

Today the meaning of "hunt" has been expanded even farther. We "hunt" for a good parking space, "hunt" for something we've lost, "hunt" for bargains when shopping, and "hunt" for a familiar face in a crowd. We even "hunt" for solutions to problems and for answers to questions. It seems as if we're always "hunting" for something.

Routine

A universal among living creatures is some degree of *routine* (pattern) in their behaviors. Humans are no different in this sense; we are creatures of habit. As distant ancestors struggled to survive, they inevitably discovered or developed more successful ways of satisfying basic needs. These quickly developed into behavioral patterns. *Routine* became common. Today most of us sleep about eight hours a day, eat three meals, and follow a certain *routine* when we get up in the morning and another pattern before going to bed. We brush our teeth and wash our body parts according to patterns. And in the work place today, *routine* enhances efficiency through regular working hours, limited job tasks for each worker—thanks to Henry Ford's assembly line, and consistent job assignments.

Family

The *family* is the most basic social group in all major societies. In modern societies, it typically includes a father role figure, a mother role figure, and their biological offspring. Of course, this wasn't always the case. In our earliest ancestors, the family did not exist. Males and females simply performed their reproductive function, then went separate ways, leaving the offspring on its own to survive as best it could. There was no bonding whatsoever. This pattern is still the norm in some species.

Sometime later, in more advanced ancestors, the first hint of the *family* appeared. Mothers bonded with their offspring and were responsible for feeding and protecting them from predators. Males, however, did not bond with the mother or offspring. They simply went from female to female to satisfy their sexual needs. The family, then, consisted of the mother and her offspring. Multiple sexual partners were the norm and were determined by chance encounters, physical dominance, and aggressiveness. This family arrangement continues to be the norm in many species.

The likely next stage in the development of the *family* appeared when individuals began forming groups because group-living offered better protection from predators and enhanced their hunting success.

Each group established its own territory and defended it against interlopers from other groups. As a matter of convenience, mature adults limited their sexual partners to the group, but probably continued to have different sexual partners within the group, still depending on physical dominance and aggressiveness. In groups which included more than one male, then, the dominant male was often the primary breeder. (In some species, the dominant male forced other males out of the group before they reached sexual maturity.) This rather primitive type of family continues to be the basic social structure in many species today, such as the baboons and lions of the African plains and the wolf of North America. It is variously referred to as a "troop," "pride," "herd," or "pack." A human variation of this ancient, rather primitive family arrangement is found in societies that permit the male to have more than one wife. Another variation, which has led to scandals from the White House on down, is practiced by those in power positions who view extra-marital affairs as one of the privileges of their status. This family arrangement has even been the practice in some close-knit groups, including religious sects. For example, according to press reports, the spiritual leader of the Branch Davidians designated himself as the primary breeder of the group.

As our ancestors evolved beyond primitive primates, two physiological changes had a profound impact on evolution of the *family:* bi-pedal locomotion (walking upright) and loss of most long body hair. Until these events occurred, the young rode on its mother's back, clinging to her body hair as she moved about in search of food and water. (Ever wonder why babies have such extraordinary gripping power?) This is still the case in today's non-human primates. But when the mother became bi-pedal and lost her long body hair, she had to hold her young in her arms as she moved about in search of food. This presented a problem: It hindered her food gathering and feeding activities. This problem was further complicated by the fact that her newborn was totally helpless at birth and matured very slowly. It couldn't be left unattended in a world of predators. If the newborn were to survive, it had to be protected and cared for for a long period. How did the mother influence the father to bond with her and their offspring? She became receptive to his sexual advances not just during her brief period of ovulation, but at other times as well. He no longer needed to pursue other females to satisfy his sexual needs. Emotional bonding usually accompanied this sexual relationship. It is no accident today, then, that women rank *seeking of security* higher than men as a reason for marriage; they are responding, at least in part, to an ancient behavioral pattern.

The *family* as we know it today, then, evolved out of the practical needs of mothers, the need to provide the most secure haven possible for raising offspring, and the male's need for a stable support system for sexual needs. It normally serves as the most secure support system against outside threats, a last bulwark against what, at times, may seem to be a cruel, hostile world. Although it has undergone some changes in America during the last three decades, the family continues to be the primary social unit in all major societies. In its traditional extended form, grandparents, aunts, uncles, cousins, and other relatives are included.

In America today, we see changes in the *family* and the reemergence of some earlier family structures. The mother-child family is becoming increasingly common as single women have children without any commitment from the fathers. (Illegitimacy is rapidly approaching one-third of all American newborns.) Divorce also contributes to reemergence of this type of family since some divorced mothers do not remarry. Divorce has also resulted in an increasingly common type of extended family that includes parents, stepparents, children, stepchildren, siblings, and half siblings—"his," "hers," "ours," and "theirs." We witness a total breakdown of the family when parents abandon their children or have them taken away by the courts because of neglect or abuse. The latest type of family to emerge openly is the gay/lesbian family.

Emotions

Emotions play an important role in daily behaviors. They are betrayed in facial expressions, body language, voice intonations, and decisions. Even dogs and cats quickly learn to associate different emotions with voice intonations. But what prompted the need for emotions? How did they evolve? Like other instincts, emotions undoubtedly originated in response to some biological need or as part of the overall struggle to survive. *Anger* and *fear* most likely developed in conjunction with the *fight/flight* instinct. They accompany, perhaps enhance, the rush of adrenaline when a threat is perceived, resulting in increased strength, speed, quickness, and the ability to react instantaneously. Likewise, *hate,* which is also accompanied by an increase in adrenaline, enables one to do things to an "enemy" that he might otherwise be unable to do. (*Hate* can, of course, be self-destructive.) On the other end of the continuum, *love* is an integral part of the bonding or attachment to a sexual partner that enhances the durability of the relationship and survival of the couple. In its most mature stage, the individual's attachment to others enables him to make sacrifices willingly, even put himself at risk for others. It is also the key bonding element between parent and child and, as such, enhances the child's chances of survival since the parent is willing to take risks to protect its child. *Compassion* and *caring* likely developed as a part of the grouping instinct in ancient times: It was in the best interest of the individual to help others survive since there was strength in numbers. These emotions are present in members of various social groups today.

Although this emotions-capability is in our genes, it should be noted that the development and display of emotions in an individual is affected to a considerable extent by one's social experiences or, more specifically, the amount of nurturing one receives during his formative years. Whether or not they develop and which develop, then, is an individual matter. A child who doesn't know love, cannot love; a child who lives in an atmosphere of hate, learns to hate. This is illustrated by the fact that adults who abuse children were nearly always abused as children themselves. The *emotions instinct,* then, provides a *potential* for development of various emotions. Which emotions develop or appear depends on the early life experiences of the individual as well as the immediate circumstances. And in time, an emotion can become institutionalized in a society or ethnic group; that is, it can become a self-perpetuating force, a way of life from one generation to the next. In today's world, for example, *hate* has become an institutionalized, festering force between groups in various countries around the world.

Reproduction

The sex drive is, of course, essential to the continuance of our species. It is one of our most powerful and pervasive instincts. It plays a highly visible, pervasive role in most societies, influencing music, art, advertising, fashions, relationships, and so on. Why? Copulation isn't just a routine event devoid of emotions such as the blinking of an eye; it is an event that normally creates strong, satisfying emotions. And once experienced, sexual activity usually becomes a regular part of the mature, healthy individual's life experiences. It isn't, then, just an event necessary to have children; it is an important element that helps bind a couple together. The sex drive is also a source of comfort and hope: It enables us to reproduce ourselves and achieve a sense of immortality since our name and genetic heritage will continue beyond death. And in our children, we have reason for tomorrow and find comfort in knowing that we will be remembered.

Campfire/Fireplace

At some point in distant times, our ancestors observed how other animals feared and avoided fire. They quickly surmised that it could protect them from fearsome creatures, especially those who hunted at night. The practice of eating animals killed by wildfires eventually led to a preference for meat cooked over a flame. (This is probably the origin of our taste for "charbroiled" meat today.) The *campfire* also became associated with full bellies and protection from the night chill. As groups huddled around it at night, it inevitably became the center of social events such as storytelling, spiritual ceremonies, and rehashing the events of the day. It became a source of comfort and reassurance. Over the millennia this association with the *campfire* became deeply etched in our psyche. Today the flame still beckons to our *prehistoric subconscious*. We continue to be drawn to the aroma, dancing flames, and snapping embers of the *campfire* or fireplace. They are commonly accepted as an essential to "camping out" and modern housing.

Spiritualism

Since the times when our earliest ancestors looked at the stars in wonder and became able to contemplate their own death well before the event, we have sought answers to questions that are not easily answered. Curiosity about ourselves and our surroundings is one of our more enduring qualities. Every society has attempted to explain who we are, why we are, why the world or universe is, and what happens to each of us when we die. They have attempted to help individuals cope with their fears and the injustices, disappointments, and hardships in life, and have offered hope for a better life tomorrow. This has usually been carried out through *spiritualism*.

Through the ages, humans have feared and worshipped the supernatural. We have looked to supernatural entities as protectors and providers, and have looked to them for answers to difficult questions. This continues today. Billions around the world, regardless of their cultural or racial heritage, continue to believe in a supreme being and, like their distant ancestors, look to it for comfort, guidance, and protection. Indeed, spiritualism is a common element in cultures around the world. Cultural groups are, in fact, commonly differentiated and described, in part, according to their unique spiritual beliefs and practices.

How did this come about? Ignorance of the causes of natural events—such as lightning and earthquakes—and associated fears undoubtedly led many of our prehistoric ancestors to believe in powerful spirits. Their tendency to attribute living qualities to natural phenomena and their need to understand their surroundings reinforced this development. Someone or something had to *cause* such events. Many concluded that Earth was their provider, the mother of life. Some cultural groups worshipped the sun. For them, it was easy to believe that it was a god because it brought light and warmth each day. It was also easy for them to interpret a solar eclipse as an omen or a sign of the sun god's displeasure. Fire, the volcano, mountain, wind, and various animals were also worshipped. A thunderstorm or the eruption of a volcano was interpreted as a sign of an angry spirit and a warning. Devastating earthquakes, floods, and other disasters were commonly interpreted as punishments for wrongdoing. To avoid punishment and ensure successful hunts and plentiful harvests, they sought to please the gods through gifts, sacrifices, and worship. Spiritualism, then, helped our distant ancestors make sense out of their world. Powerful spirits or gods controlled the uncontrollable and explained the unexplainable. They provided answers to questions that could not be otherwise explained.

Our ancestors' awareness of their own mortality and their survival instinct, however, were undoubtedly key factors in the development of *spiritualism*. When they became capable of contemplating their own death and its finality, their survival instinct and intellect drove them to seek ways of escaping it. What might show the way? The most powerful forces known were the spirits—the sun, the mountain, the wind, the thunderstorm, the earth itself. The spirits provided plentiful rain and food and could surely show the way. How did they elicit the assistance of the spirits? They first had to convince them that they were *worthy* and deserving to live beyond this world. How was this accomplished? By providing the spirits with gifts, making sacrifices, rituals, and other practices, and, significantly, by living their lives in accordance with what was "handed down" through spiritual intermediaries. Such demonstrations of respect and loyalty, according to the intermediaries, enhanced their chances of entering the "afterlife."

"Revelations" by "chosen ones" later reinforced many older beliefs, and provided a more specific basis for the development of today's modern religions. Revelations spelled out appropriate beliefs, attitudes, rituals, and practices. In most religions, spirits became singular and personal. This more personal god was aware of each person and, when called upon, responded to the condition and needs of each who was deserving. Individuals, then, didn't have to rely on spiritual intermediaries to communicate with the Great Spirit, God, Allah, etc. Appropriate beliefs, attitudes, and practices eventually became institutionalized as religions. Today, they commonly promote respect for a deity and a desire to please it in songs, rituals, chants, and symbolic or real sufferings and sacrifices. A core belief in most modern religions promises the individual that he will survive his greatest fear, his own death: If he lives in accordance with prescribed beliefs, he will rise to a level of "goodness" that will be rewarded with a *good* afterlife. Otherwise, he will either have no afterlife, or his afterlife will be one of perpetual punishment. *Spiritualism,* and the promise of a good afterlife in particular, as a result, have served as rather powerful social controls through the millennia.

Understandably, those who served as spiritual intermediaries were accorded positions of status and power. Spiritual leaders continue to wield considerable power in most societies. They typically play a significant role in determining the morality of a cultural group—what is *right* and what is *wrong,* what is *good* and what is *evil,* and how we are supposed to be.

Why, with our considerable body of scientific knowledge and our growing understanding of the immensity and complexity of the universe, does *spiritualism* continue to thrive? In part because we are still inclined to think that things must have a beginning and an end, and that all things have a purpose. Most believe that something or someone far superior must be responsible for the existence of the universe. The problem is, it's really not possible to comprehend absolutely nothing—not empty space, just nothing—which, according to some, is supposed to have been the case before the "Big Bang." Someone or something *had* to be there in the beginning. And so it was written, *In the beginning...* Of course our fear of death and our survival instinct still compel most to hope and believe in an afterlife. This explains why most of us try to make contact with a spiritual entity when death seems imminent. It also explains why there really aren't any atheists in foxholes. Our refusal to "let go" of deceased loved ones and the desire to see them again also compel many to believe in a supreme being and an afterlife. Disappointments and the perceived unfairness of life also continue. Surely, there must be something better. And so we believe, hope, and pray. Why does spiritualism continue? It is in our genes because it is a consequence of our consciousness and ability to think.

Aesthetic Expression

Give a four-year-old crayons and paper and he'll spend hours drawing and coloring. Play music that has a distinct beat, and a two-year-old will smile and move to the beat of the music. And what small child doesn't like, "Once upon a time..."? Appreciation of the aesthetics is in our genes. Ancient drawings in caves and sculptures excavated from ancient ruins have revealed that our early ancestors expressed themselves aesthetically. Then, as now, such expression apparently was a source of enjoyment. Indeed, all cultural groups express themselves aesthetically. And since it is a universal, cultural groups are identified in part by the unique way they express themselves aesthetically. Each is somewhat unique in its music, dance, painting, sculptures, literature, and theater. The aesthetics continue to be immensely popular today: Billions are spent annually on sculptures, paintings, music, and the other aesthetics. Even customized cars become works of art. This instinct is also closely tied to the desire to achieve immortality: As we express ourselves aesthetically, we leave behind parts of us—which will enable others to understand and remember us individually and collectively.

Language

Animals typically produce sounds to communicate with each other. These sounds are related to a variety of needs, such as feeding, control, location and group maintenance, mating, caring for the young, and expression of emotions such as distress and anger. We, too, produce sounds to communicate with each other—for many of the same reasons. When does this begin? Like the newly hatched or newborn of other animals, a baby cries immediately after birth to announce his arrival. He then begins differentiating cries to communicate hunger, illness, need for a diaper change, or need for comforting physical contact. Mothers learn quickly to distinguish one cry from another cry.

Regardless of their cultural and linguistic setting, children then proceed through a common pattern of language acquisition. Each child begins producing words and sentences peculiar to his language environment, beginning with holophrastic speech (one word as a sentence as in, "Eat!" meaning, "I want to eat."), then proceeding to telegraphic speech (two or more words as a sentence as in, "Me want eat!" meaning, "I want to eat."). The child eventually develops a considerable vocabulary and an ability to construct an infinite number of "complete" sentences that serve a variety of needs. Language acquisition is, of course, contingent upon a child's exposure to language; without exposure, he continues with grunts and other primitive sounds to communicate with others. But the *capacity* to produce language sounds and acquire language is innate. And since exposure to language is normal, children normally acquire and develop adequate facility with their native language.

Play

Observation of young animals, regardless of species, reveals that play occupies a considerable amount of their time. This is also the case in our species. Children, beginning at an early age, participate in a variety of games, have imaginary playmates, and act out adult roles. Why do they play? It helps them develop the physical abilities necessary for adult life and develop some understanding about adult roles and responsibilities. Of course, children don't have a monopoly on play. Adults also spend considerable time (and money) in play activities, such as golfing, fishing, and skiing.

Concluding Thoughts About Their Role

As noted earlier, instincts have their origins in our earliest ancestors millions of years ago. They were essential for survival then, and continue to be powerful forces. Even after reaching social maturity, instincts may emerge under certain circumstances and dominate behaviors, sometimes resulting in what appears to be irrational behavior. Otherwise, there would be no unwanted pregnancies, no disputes between neighbors that lead to violent acts, and there would be no shootings in love triangles. We would always make sensible decisions and settle differences in nonviolent ways. But we don't. Unseen forces within sometimes compel us to take risks and do irrational, destructive things. Threatening situations often make things worse. How so? The greater the threat, the greater the likelihood that rational thought and a sense of right and wrong will be displaced by primitive survival forces, resulting in poor decisions and destructive actions. Like the horse that refuses to leave its stall inside a burning barn, this explains, in some cases, why the abused spouse or child, instead of pressing charges, clings to her abuser; she is responding to the *family* instinct, trying to maintain a semblance of security in what is normally our most protective social unit—even in the face of physical violence. She may also be responding to her *territorial* instinct, clinging to familiar surroundings rather than fleeing to the uncertainties of the world beyond. It also explains the initial rage and desire of parents to attack the killer of their child and the urge of a husband to kill the individual who raped his wife.

There are also examples throughout history that illustrate the presence of these instincts. Most apparent are the struggles for dominance or control—wars of conquest, wars for revenge, and wars for independence; patriotic wars and trade wars. Consider the development of the Roman Empire. The Spanish conquest of the Incas. The War Over Jenkins' Ear. Nazi Germany. Countless political assassinations. The Gulf War. As a matter of fact, the history of major human events is comprised to a considerable extent of actions, reactions, and counteractions in an endless struggle for *power*. Apparently, *the beast within* forever demands a major part in the making of history, and it increasingly seems to be getting its way—from the streets of America to the reappearance of ethnic tribalism in the world today. These events serve not only as chilling reminders of our primitive heritage, but also as evidence of the continuing struggle with ourselves.

Some of the worst violence has been carried out *in the name of God*. Consider the Crusades. Warriors and soldiers invoking the strength and protection of God. Car bombings by religious fundamentalists in the Middle East. Shootings of doctors at abortion clinics. Countless conquests to "convert" others—even when it means killing many of them. War in Bosnia between Muslims and Christians. Ongoing clashes between Hindus and Moslems in India. These events, of course, should be interpreted more correctly as examples of the lust for power or resources by those in positions of authority and their lack of respect for human differences—not as examples of destructive religions. They also stand as examples of our inability or unwillingness to settle conflicts through non-violent means, and as examples of misplaced priorities or moral elitism.

Primitive instincts do not, of course, explain all violent behaviors. Abnormal mental conditions are sometimes contributing factors. Deranged individuals do commit crimes. Paranoid individuals, for example, harbor delusions and irrational suspicions that sometimes result in violent retaliatory acts. Others, whose mistrust has some rational basis, sometimes experience exaggerated suspicions to the point that they act to protect themselves or what they believe in. Those who suffer from post-traumatic stress disorder (PTSD), a pathological disorder, also may react violently out of fear when they encounter a triggering device that causes them to "flashback" to the trauma. But instincts even play a part in these cases. How so? The perception of a serious threat to one's well-being normally triggers various survival reactions, including fear. Whether the threat is real or imagined is irrelevant. It is the *perception* of the threat that matters.

Irrational, destructive behaviors also have been defended before courts as cases of "temporary" insanity. Indeed, it is widely understood that individuals sometimes commit violent acts during "fits" of rage or extreme anger. Jilted spouses and lovers, for example, often either fantasize about or carry out vengeful acts—which occasionally result in convictions. Some contend that all divorcing couples "go a little crazy" and do things they wouldn't ordinarily do. (Countless police officers would agree.) Should periods of extreme emotional distress that trigger unusual violent behaviors be defined as "temporary" insanity? In most cases, probably not. One thing is certain: Primitive, reactionary forces within us are most likely to erupt in situations when our personal sense of security is seriously threatened.

Paradoxically, instincts make it possible to live, yet threaten our existence. They enable us to reproduce ourselves, and drive us to destroy each other. They are the forces behind our laughter and tears, our loyalties and jealousies. Uncontrollable rage and deep compassion. Wars of conquest and great achievements in medical science. Children who are deeply loved and abortions. Our need to explore and understand the universe and pollution of the environment.

DIFFERENT BEHAVIOR MODES

Apparently, humans can operate in different behavioral modes and shift from one to another. What emerges depends on the circumstances. We may behave as rational, inquisitive, creative, and compassionate beings; under stress we may behave as emotionally-charged destructive creatures. We may also behave as regimented beings that cling to habits and routines. What accounts for these different behavioral modes?

Hart postulated in his *three-brain concept* that these sharp distinctions in behavior can be attributed to different parts of the brain or, as he put it, to our three different brains.[1] We shift from one brain to another, depending upon the degree of felt threat. He explained that our most primitive brain, the brain stem, developed millions of years ago in ancestors that were much simpler life forms. In addition to physiological functions like regulation of heartbeat and body temperature, it is the source of our most primitive instincts such as reproduction, territorialism, aggression, and fight/flight. Behaviors, including reflexes, are instantaneous and automatic in this mode of operation. No thinking is required. Regular seating patterns at the dinner table, routines, and panic reactions have their origins in this brain. "Lower" animals, such as chickens, operate only in this mode, adapting to the environment and reacting to immediate conditions rather than shaping the environment to their needs. Although they can be conditioned through stimulus-response training to do some unnatural things such as "play" a child's toy piano, their capacity for real learning is quite limited.

Our somewhat more advanced brain, equivalent to the "limbic system," developed later and was added to the brain stem, resulting in a more advanced form of life. This brain is less rigid, and it is preoccupied with emotions. It is the source of emotional responses to various events and conditions.

The largest portion of our brain, the cerebrum, developed still later and was added over those structures described above. It is by far the most complex and has a great capacity for learning. It is the source of the ability to think and act rationally, our inquisitiveness, aesthetic expression, speech, and problem solving abilities. (Ever wonder why someone became speechless when he became very frightened?) The cerebrum is also the source of our ability to adapt the environment to our desires. It is the source of all academic and vocational learning, and technological advancements. Although it works much more slowly than those brain structures that developed earlier, it enables us to be highly adaptable, problem-solving beings.

Whether we accept this *three-brain concept* or not, the fact remains that ordinary people leading ordinary lives can and do exhibit a considerable range of emotional states and behaviors. It isn't a matter of sanity or insanity; it is simply the way we are. When our

---

[1] Leslie A. Hart, "The Three-Brain Concept and the Classroom," *Phi Delta Kappan*; March, 1981, pp. 504-506.

comfortable self-respect is seriously threatened, when achievement of cherished goals is threatened, we may react emotionally and irrationally. Most of us, for example, have heard or read about an individual who reacted violently when he was terminated from his job—whether it was a postal worker or someone in a corporate office. Likewise, there's the situation compounded by the dark side of the maternal instinct: the mother who, after hearing her child tell how his teacher mistreated him, shifts into a defensive attack mode even *before* talking with the teacher and angrily confronts the teacher because she views this as an attack on *her* competence as a parent. The same mechanism is apparent when a parent, upon being told by a neighbor of her child's misbehavior, interprets this as an attack on her competence as a parent and counterattacks to defend not her child's alleged innocence but the family reputation and prestige in the community. This counterattack may extend into the community with an attempt to discredit the neighbor with others.

A More Basic Perspective

If we are to deal effectively with our problems today, especially those related to relationships with one another, we must recognize and accept the fact that the beast and warrior still live within us. And this will not change. They are in our genes. They are the source of our aggressions, violent reactions when "vital" interests are threatened, hate, and demands for revenge. Newspapers and the network news remind us daily of their presence.

Of course, we are not just primitive beings whose behaviors are dominated by prehistoric survival instincts. We are more. Much more. History and the desire for a better world also reveal us to be caring, creative, and compassionate social beings who usually behave toward one another in sensible, considerate ways. And we are inquisitive creatures who enjoy exploring the unknown and solving problems.

But in today's world, where lethal weapons are becoming increasingly available, the most pressing problem confronting humanity must surely be: how to minimize the destruction that we inflict on ourselves as a species, as a society, and as individuals.

The challenge to society, then, is as it has always been: to domesticate this beast within, to create sensible beings who are "in tune" culturally and socially, beings whose behaviors are dominated by rational thought processes and mutual respect rather than by primitive, reactionary and sometimes destructive instincts. This means, among other things, transforming selfish, demanding newborns who are prone to aggression to get what they want into beings who understand and appreciate the needs and rights of others.

And the challenge to each of us remains: to develop the ability to maintain self-control and behave in ways that are socially and culturally constructive.

These are great challenges, especially since they cannot be accomplished or solved "once and for all." They are endless tasks. For each new generation and for each of us as we begin life.

Chapter II

Taming Of The Beast

To educate a person in mind and not in morals is to educate a menace to society. — Theodore Roosevelt

If we are to domesticate this beast within, what then is required? Many cry for stricter laws and stricter enforcement of laws. They argue that more police, more judges, longer sentences, and more jails will solve crime problems and make streets safe again. But will these measures really solve our problems? Do societies normally control the primitive, potentially violent forces within their members just by putting more and more police on the streets and building more and more jails? Of course not.

Social order and social compatibility are predicated on individuals who have internalized, for the most part, the prevailing values and behavioral code of their society. This means that they don't just *accept* the behavioral code; they *believe* that what is expected of them is *right*. And they behave accordingly. In a very real sense, then, it is a part of them. Mere toleration of constraints or behavioral standards is not enough. Nor is fear of punishment.

Why is it important that individuals internalize the values and behavioral expectations of their society? Values and behavioral standards are part of the glue that holds a culture or society together. How so? They identify the importance of things and prescribe what is and what is not acceptable behavior in that setting. And in time, they become part of the traditions and institutions of a society, affecting not only what members believe to be important, but also how individuals live together and express themselves. They become, then, part of the cultural heritage passed on from one generation to the next.

Internalization of the code is also important because the code includes rules that govern how individuals are to interact and processes for settling inevitable conflicts. As individuals internalize the code, they learn how to interact with each other, and violent conflicts are minimized. Many even strive to "do good," to make life more just, meaningful, and worthwhile for others—whether in the community or in the world. So we have volunteer community beautification groups, the United Way, Habitat for Humanity, and legal assistance programs for the poor. The Lions Club, scholarships, adoptive parents, and organ donor programs. These are clear reflections of our sense of morality. Fortunately, nearly all of us develop some limited sense of morality because our socio-cultural environment fosters development of a sense of right and wrong. It includes rather powerful social and legal controls that can bring considerable pressure to bear on the individual who deviates.

In today's modern, densely populated societies, control of primitive, often violent urges is especially important. So is cooperation. Of course this was not always the case. Individual families on the frontier produced many of the basic stuffs that they needed and were independent to a considerable extent. They had to be. There were few close neighbors, and the few manufactured goods available required travel by horse to a distant trading post or to a general store in a small community. But in today's modern societies, the conveniences of urban living have drawn us close together, and we have become very dependent upon each other as we have become specialized in work. We *have* to interact more and cooperate more not only because of our close proximity to each other, but also because we produce many essential things for each other. Social order and management of potentially violent instincts, then, are essential to the survival of modern societies.

Of course humans are not unique in this respect. Other animal species normally construct social order and display various behavioral patterns and rituals that are designed to minimize violent conflicts among members. In addition to the physical attributes peculiar to a species, they are, simply put, what makes a cat a cat and a dog a dog. These behavioral codes are geared toward survival and determine behaviors in all critical areas, including feeding, reproduction, play, shelter, power within the group, and escaping threats. The wolf pack, for example, is based on certain behavioral patterns and ritual behaviors that are peculiar to wolves. And like other species, the pack or family structure is based on a *pecking order*. This pecking order is usually determined by the sex and physical abilities of each member, and is signaled by various dominance and submission behaviors. Among humans, this tendency to establish a pecking order or hierarchy is apparent in all types of groups, whether it be a family, a gang, a corporation, or a government. Rank or status is apparent, for example, in the way we dress; in the, "Please rise," when the judge enters the courtroom; in one's position in a procession such as a parade or funeral; in perks or privileges for leaders; and in the way we address each other, such as *Mr..., Madam Chairman, Dr...,* and *President....*

THE HUMAN DIFFERENCE

How is the behavioral code of each species usually passed on from one generation to the next? Among most species, instincts play the major role. That is, as the newborn (or newly hatched) begins life and grows, its behaviors appear spontaneously with little or no prompting from others. A newly hatched chick automatically begins scratching and pecking at the soil, a newborn killer whale surges to the surface for its first breath, and newly hatched sea turtles scamper toward the surf. Among those species where the young must *learn* some aspects of their behavioral code, it is usually taught to the young through parent modeling.

The Role of Learning

While the behaviors of "lower" animals are largely dictated by instincts, that is, behavioral patterns that are genetically encoded before birth, the origin of our behaviors is more complex. In humans, *learning* plays a considerably greater role in the preparation of each new generation for life. But like other species where learning plays a role, parents normally play the most important part, with the surrounding tribe or community playing a close second. For it is within the family and supporting community where children learn the finer points about being human, and how to function as a member of a human social group. Two key functions of the family and community, then, are (1) to help the child internalize the values and behavioral code appropriate for a given socio-cultural environment through use of acceptable techniques, and (2) to maintain the necessary social and legal institutions and processes for reinforcing those learnings and keeping our destructive forces, our "dark side," in check. This isn't easy, nor is society always successful. As noted in Chapter I, some individuals, for a variety of reasons, fall outside the parameters of what society has legally defined as acceptable behavior and commit serious legal infractions. Prisons are overfilled with them. But most individuals, despite an occasional minor social or legal indiscretion, learn how to "get along." That is, they conform to the general expectations of society and lead what is considered to be "normal" lives.

Our instincts, then, are supplemented to a greater extent by what *is learned* after birth. (Our large cerebrum makes this possible.) And what is learned depends upon each individual's specific cultural environment. As societies vary, so too will customs, traditions, values, and morals. Each will have its own unique beliefs and practices. For example, in the traditional culture of Saudi Arabia, it is highly inappropriate for a woman to expose her face in public or wear facial makeup. All these things the young must learn.

Coping With Our Prehistoric Heritage

A society or culture is, in itself, a control structure. Indeed, as a social group grows and matures into a culture, it creates a rather elaborate code that prescribes how members should and should not behave. This code is embodied in commonly accepted beliefs, laws, and traditions, and provides guidelines for interactions of members. It defines what is *right* and what is *wrong*, and serves as the basis for morality and justice in that environment. Processes for training the young, rewarding those who do well, and punishing those who deviate are established, and institutions, such as the *family, traditions, schools, religious centers,* and *court systems*, promote the continuance of the culture. Impulsive, violent behaviors of *the beast within* are discouraged. Specific control techniques, such as rewards, social ostracism, and detention, are commonly employed.

These social and legal controls must, of course, be widely embraced by members of society. Why? It is essential to reasonably harmonious relationships among members, especially in societies composed of different cultural groups. Otherwise, conflicts between society and those who consider the expectations to be unacceptable are inevitable. How do societies achieve widespread acceptance of social and legal controls? Each individual and each cultural group must be represented to some extent in the broad expectations of society and must feel they are reasonable. In order for this to occur, the values and behavioral standards must reflect, to some extent, the expectations of the various cultural groups within it. That is, they must be comprised of elements common to the various groups, and each group must feel that it has an acceptable level of ownership. Behavioral standards, at least those written into laws, must also be applied equally to all groups. Individuals from different cultural backgrounds must have equal rights, and penalties for deviant behaviors must be applied equally. Otherwise, discord and cries of discrimination are inevitable. Harmony and social control are further promoted by achievement of an acceptable balance between individual freedoms, on the one hand, and reasonable conformity to societal expectations. This allows members from different cultural groups to still express themselves in their unique customs and traditions.

Societies also commonly try to accommodate violent tendencies by establishing controlled environments where these forces can be safely vented. This explains why we have football, chess matches, boxing, hockey, bullfighting, professional wrestling, hunting, cockfighting... Ever notice how even "sophisticated" celebrities are at ringside to enjoy boxing matches? Yes, even they find the adrenaline "high" irresistible. And if the fighters don't really "mix it up," spectators jeer loudly because the greatest thrill is a bloody knockout punch that nearly tears a guy's head off! Millions enjoy these activities. For example, in Texas alone, 586,348 hunters spent 5,398,874 days in 1991 in pursuit of deer.[2] These figures do not take into account the number of illegal hunters or hunters in pursuit of other "game" animals. And an increasing number of us "hunt" each other in wooded areas with paintball guns and in airplane "dogfights" on weekends. (This brings to mind one of my most memorable short stories from my high school days, Richard Connell's *The Most Dangerous Game*. Connell apparently had a good understanding of one aspect of human nature!) Thrill-seekers flirt with death in skydiving, rock climbing, and similar high-risk activities; millions enjoy action adventure movies and horror movies; and children eagerly anticipate Halloween. What do they have in common? They are all controlled outlets for powerful forces within. Some allow us to satisfy needs vicariously, while others are *danger and escape games* that allow direct participation in controlled, safe environments. Of course humans aren't entirely unique in this respect. Other animals have their own games. They engage in mock battles and other non-lethal ritualistic behaviors as part of an overall scheme to establish and maintain a pecking order, and thereby minimize injuries to each other.

Camping out, outdoor photography, bird watching, and the concern for wildlife are also based on our prehistoric heritage from the savanna and forest. So is the attraction of the fireplace and the

---

[2] Ray Sasser, "Buck Fever: Passion for Deer Hunting is Part of Texas Heritage," *Texas Parks and Wildlife*; October, 1992, p.8.

campfire. We enjoy the dancing of the flames, the snapping and popping of the embers, and the aroma of the smoke, but, as noted in Chapter I, there are deeper reasons for the attraction of the campfire and fireplace. We are, in part, still creatures of the forest who, by the millions, look to the outdoors—whether it is camping, hunting, hiking or fishing—as an escape from pressures of modern living.

As noted earlier, however, even with these controls and outlets in place, there is always a chance that some instincts will emerge in socially unacceptable ways. For a variety of reasons, we simply are not always rational beings; the "dark side" sometimes surfaces and dominates our behaviors. It seems more and more of us, for whatever reason, go beyond vicarious experiences and simulations, and act out violent urges.

An issue gripping many is: Does vicarious participation in boxing events, violent acts on TV, and similar aggressive activities increase or decrease the probability that the individual will act out his anti-social urges? More specifically, does endless exposure to violent acts increase or decrease the probability that those in the audience will act out similar internal forces? If it depends on the individual, at what point does participation in these activities as a means of *satisfying* one's instincts end, and *enhancement* of these destructive forces begin?

CREATING SOCIALLY COMPATIBLE INDIVIDUALS

As noted earlier, a cultural group can be described, in part, by its values and morality because they are integral parts of the customs and traditions that distinguish it from other cultural groups. And as values and morality change, so too does a cultural group. The transmission of values and morals from one generation to the next, then, is crucial to the continued existence of that cultural group.

Responsible Agents

What agents are responsible for passing on the values and morality to the next generation? Traditional agents have included:

— Family (especially parents, siblings, relatives)
— Friends
— Peer Group
— Spiritual Institutions
— School (curricular materials, faculty)
— Advertising

— Entertainment (movies, television, music, literature, etc.)
— Prestige people
— Organizations that promote development of values, character, and citizenship (Girl Scouts, etc.)

Which are the most influential in forming an individual's moral values? Ordinarily, parents, siblings, and friends—in that order. But the impact of the various agents will vary, depending on the unique circumstances of each child, the child's developmental level, and how well the child *likes* a person. For example, an abusive parent may have less impact than a favorite grandparent. Or a favorite teacher or coach may play a significant role. Consider the impact that Abraham Lincoln had on the values of millions. And Jesus Christ. Popular athletes and other celebrities also may exert influence. (Otherwise, why would so many receive millions for endorsing and advertising all kinds of products?) And a fourteen-year-old will nearly always be more concerned with the opinions and tastes of his peers than with those of his parents because of the great peer pressure to conform, especially among girls.

Techniques for Transmitting Values & Morals

What techniques are employed to transmit values and morals from one generation to the next? Traditionally, a combination of modeling (role models), reinforcement (pleasant responses to desirable behaviors), and punishment (unpleasant responses to undesirable behaviors) has been employed to exert the desired social control and cause the next generation to internalize the desired values and morals. Specific techniques include:

— Role models/examples of desired value/behavior
— Admonitions to do as told
— Induction (reasoning, explaining consequences of choices)
— Limiting choices to those that are acceptable
— Cultural and religious dogma
— Study of value/moral-oriented materials and lessons in school
— Appeals to conscience
— Threats (fear of punishment)
— Physical punishment
— Reward/recognition of those who exhibit desired behaviors
— Withdrawal or withholding of desired privileges
— Ridicule of those who exhibit undesired behaviors

— Inclusion/exclusion from social group (silent treatment," "time out," "go to your room," organizations, and so on)
— Ceremonial rituals, myths, folktales
— Restitution to victim
— Community service
— Compulsory enrollment in "rehab" program

The Onset of Training

Each of us, as noted above, is born in a socio-cultural environment. And each society includes nurturing and socializing processes that are designed to help the individual become an integral part of society—and thereby minimize conflicts with other members of society. When does socialization begin? Virtually the first day of life. As the child proceeds through the socialization process, he encounters the needs and expectations of others and begins learning "rules" about how to share, what is fair, and what is important—the beginnings of values and morality. These rules focus on a variety of matters, such as, "Wash your hands," taking turns; no hitting, biting, scratching, or spitting; asking for something instead of just taking it, "respecting" adults, and, "Don't pick your nose."

Initially, the young child is completely self-centered. All that he sees is part of him; that is, the world is an extension of him. His behaviors are driven by survival instincts—and, as a matter of survival, he is selfish and demanding. The *cry* instinct is first to appear, and is used to communicate various needs to providers—whether it is for nourishment, a need for a diaper change, or attention to an illness. Emotions are directly linked to satisfaction of these needs. Angry cries and temper tantrums may erupt to persuade caretakers to attend his needs. Why are these sounds so annoying to us adults? Crying sounds were developed to perfection over the millennia as the most effective way a baby can behave to get others to satisfy his needs. Until a child begins acquiring language, they are his most effective means of controlling others. He will continue to use them as long as they are effective—even after he has learned to talk. The cry is soon supplemented with the smile as a means of communicating emotions to others.

Some primitive survival instincts are most exposed during this early period. Why? The child is the least inhibited during this time because he has yet to internalize any constraints imposed by society; that is, he is least affected by those outside forces that socialization will impose on him as he proceeds through *the formative years*.

The young child soon begins to distinguish himself from his immediate environment, including caretakers and siblings, and begins pursuing his *place* in the family. As he does this, he adds another dimension to his *self*. He becomes *others-aware*. That is, he becomes aware of the separateness of others and, significantly, their competing needs. But he still selfishly demands that caretakers satisfy *his* needs—not those of siblings, because he is unable to appreciate the condition or needs of others. He competes with siblings for parental attention in a variety of ways as he seeks to satisfy his emotional, physical, and social needs. Just listen how often four-year-olds fight about what is "mine."

Although a child is initially unable to appreciate the needs or condition of others during this period, he soon learns to negotiate with them to get what he wants. He helps others, then, as a means of helping himself. For example, a child may propose to let a playmate play with his toy truck so he can play with the friend's toy airplane. At this stage he is concerned with his playmate's condition only to the extent that it will affect his chances of getting what he wants. Only later, after beginning to develop the ability to empathize, is he able to understand and unselfishly respond to the needs of others.

Development of altruism should, and normally does, begin quite early. How does the child begin to acquire altruistic characteristics? By observing altruistic behaviors of significant others, most often those of his mother, and by being the object of altruistic behaviors. Gentle, loving responses to his needs by others, especially his parents, make impressions on his character that will last a lifetime. How do we know when a child is developing altruism? By observing his behaviors. Most of us, for example, have observed a young child try to console a crying baby sister by giving her a toy or a bottle.

Does this mean sibling rivalry ends with the development of altruism? No. On the contrary, *competition* and *territorial* instincts often fuel sibling rivalries even into adulthood. But the child's development of altruism is important since it acts as a counterweight to self-serving, anti-social tendencies, and because it is a key element in the socialized human being.

As the child grows toward adolescence, he becomes *others-oriented*, or more concerned with how he fits in with others. (Just watch junior high students.) He strives to be *like* his peers in dress, speech, interests, and morality (beliefs about *right* and *wrong*). Being *fair* becomes a cornerstone of his morality. (Of course their ideas about *fairness* don't always coincide with those of their parents.) Just listen how often adolescents use the words "fair" and "unfair." This development of "fairness" is a direct result of our dependency on each other in social groups: As we negotiate social and economic relationships, we inevitably develop a sense of fairness.

As values and morals are internalized during the socialization process, they increasingly affect decisions; sometimes, unfortunately, they are even sources of conflicts between individuals or between nations. How so? Adverse emotional reactions and conflicts arise when one party violates a strongly held belief of another party about fairness or what is right, or impedes one's achievement of a "rightful" goal. These conflicts may focus on a territorial dispute such as who was "first" to claim a parking space or "ask a girl out," a disagreement over "fairness" in trade relations between nations, marital infidelity, a deserved job promotion denied, or a parent's objection to a child's attending a rock concert. Fortunately, a system of values and morals normally includes mechanisms for resolving conflicts in mutually acceptable, non-violent ways. Whether or not these mechanisms are employed is another matter—and depends on a variety of factors, such as our respect for each other, the ability to maintain self-composure under pressure, our moral maturity, and the strength of our commitment to conflict resolution through negotiation and compromise.

Of those elements, moral maturity is crucial. We've all heard someone say, "There ought to be a law," and, "Let's make a rule." And we've heard of "going along with the crowd," "an eye for an eye," the *Golden Rule*, and the *Ten Commandments*. These are control referents. They are linked to beliefs about acceptable behavior and about punishments for wrongdoing. They are also indicators of different levels of moral maturity. Other common comments such as, "Everybody else is doing it," "What's in it for me?" and, "Just don't get caught," are also indicators of moral maturity.

VALUES, MORALS & PRIORITIES

In today's world there are countless examples on the individual level and in world politic that one can cite to strengthen the argument that we probably won't survive ourselves. Development and application of technology for destroying each other does indeed seem to present a very real threat to our continued existence. Whether humanity self-destructs remains an open question. If we are to survive ourselves, respect for universal human rights and dignity must be the foundation for such a world. To do so, however, we first need to understand the nature of *values, morals,* and *priorities.* What exactly are values? And what are morals? How do they differ from each other? And how do values and morals differ from priorities?

What They Are

Values and morals are not things or behaviors, but pure abstractions, existing only in the mind. They are beliefs about *right* and *wrong* and the importance of things. Although they can't be seen or touched, everyday behaviors betray their presence. Values and morals are learned according to one's specific experiences, direct and indirect, and, of course, reflect one's social and cultural heritage. And since family experiences typically play the major role in the early formation of values and morals, they necessarily reflect the uniqueness of each individual's family background. Once formed, values and morals tend to be resistant to change.

But values and morals are not just beliefs. They constitute the core of the affective domain, impacting everything said and done. Opinions, attitudes, and decisions about lifestyles, friendships, careers, and issues are directly related to them. They also serve as filters through which all experiences are interpreted, including behaviors of others. Once established, then, values and morals predispose us to behave in certain ways and determine how we expect others to behave. Those who violate common expectations of society are punished.

Values and morals can also provide a rational basis for living. When clearly established, they provide a framework for behaving consistently and functioning as an integral part of a social structure. They give purpose and meaning to life by providing a foundation for setting goals and a framework for organizing all that we do. Once values and morals are clearly established and culturally compatible, they serve as a foundation for deciding what our goals should be. This enables us to make decisions that we can live with.

Differences in values and morals are often the source of conflicts between cultural groups and individuals. How so? Conflicts often occur because of the tendency to project our values and expectations about right and wrong on others. That is, we tend to expect others to believe and behave as we do. Conflicts also occur when we fail to realize that values or morals of others differ from ours, when they are rejected outright, or when the right to hold different values or morals is denied. Some will go to extremes to impose their beliefs on others.

How They Differ

In brief, a value is a belief about the importance or relative importance of something. It may focus on a material object, a behavior, a goal, or a character trait. Values answer the question: What is important? They enable us to establish the general importance of specific things but *not* their "goodness" or social acceptability. Values merely serve to identify those things, beliefs, and actions that are important. They serve as an important element in establishing order and setting goals, and provide a basis for setting priorities by specifying the general importance of things that are valued or considered to be important. Value beliefs predispose us to act in certain ways to the extent that a belief about the importance of something is weighed in a decision.

And morals? A moral is a belief that establishes a standard about what is socially responsible and constructive in society. It focuses on behaviors, attitudes, character traits, and moral issues such as capital punishment. Morals influence what we do and with whom we associate, even how we dress. They serve as principles that enable individuals to judge the difference between right and wrong, and good and bad. Morals answer the questions: Is it right? Is it fair? Is it the right thing to do? They enable us, then, to judge whether or not a behavior is right or fair according to those standards that have been adopted. Although these standards may vary somewhat from one individual to the next, there is necessarily considerable common ground among individuals who grow up in a given culture—otherwise, the socio-cultural fabric is seriously weakened.

Morals, then, are the foundation for accepted definitions of fairness, justice and respect. They guide actions, help establish consistency in actions, and predispose individuals to behave in socially acceptable ways. They serve as guidelines for human interactions and relationships and, as such, provide a framework for etiquette and ethics in social relationships, business transactions, civic affairs...all types of interactions. Morals enable individuals to screen their values, that is, judge if something valued is right. A society, then, can't exist on material values alone. There must also be an accepted system of morality.

And priorities? A priority is the importance or relative importance placed on a choice among choices in a given situation. Priorities, then, answer the questions: How important is it in this situation? What is most important in this situation? When confronted with these choices? Setting priorities enables us to make decisions when confronted with two or more goals/choices/problems that need attending—and decide which to attend to first.

Setting priorities is an important ingredient in effective planning and problem solving. It enables us to weigh the relative attractiveness of choices when resources are limited in a given situation; it enables us to organize or rank choices according to immediate needs as circumstances vary. Setting priorities, then, provides operational flexibility as values are applied in daily affairs.

How They Are Related

Decisions, no matter how trivial, reveal something about values, morals, and priorities. How so? We prioritize tasks that need attending in daily affairs. These tasks are directly related to goals and beliefs which, in turn, reflect what is valued and what is believed to be *right*. Values, morals, and priorities, then, are inexorably intertwined in human behaviors. There can be no morals without values, and priorities can't be set without first having determined those things that are important. It is possible, however, for an individual to have values and priorities but be amoral—that is, not have a sense of right and wrong. But these are rare cases. Any time a group forms, understandings about the roles, organization, and interactions of members will follow. That is, members (or a domineering leader) will develop a code of conduct that defines roles, the power structure, and how members are to behave. Members who deviate will be "wrong." Even ruthless drug dealers and gang leaders establish a code that defines what is "right" and "wrong" in the group. The problem is, what a drug leader or gang defines as right and wrong is usually not compatible with or society as a whole.

The label *moral values* is often heard in daily affairs. What does it mean? Like values that focus on material matters, morals are typically weighted in terms of importance, with some considered to be more important than others. For example, even though each is considered to be "wrong," murder is considered to be a more serious crime than robbery because society places a higher value on life than on material possessions. Value differentials determine the "seriousness" of the crime and are the basis for different punishments. A *moral value*, then, is a belief that identifies a desirable behavior *and* establishes its relative importance among other morals. It may serve as a guideline for constructive relationships between individuals, among members in a group, members of the community, or members

The Challenge of the New Millennium

of a whole society. In any case, it identifies a behavior (or misbehavior if stated in the negative) that is understood to have some degree of social and moral significance in the community or society.

The Importance of Morality

As noted in Chapter I, to some individuals, *right* and *wrong* are determined by what they *value* and what they can get by with. If they *want* what someone else has, taking it is okay if they don't get caught. The impact of their actions on victims is irrelevant. If a victim is injured during the process, it's his own fault; he shouldn't have resisted.

Apparently, an individual, as noted earlier, can internalize values but be amoral. He can be educated intellectually (or, for that matter, be uneducated) but be devoid of a conscience. This is a dangerous situation, as even Theodore Roosevelt noted, "To educate a person in mind and not in morals is to educate a menace to society." The individual without a conscience or sense of morality has no real capacity for relating to the condition of others or caring for them. Such a person typically displays behavior that is not only completely self-serving but also socially and culturally destructive. Hitler, for example, had a clear set of values and goals, but his morality, his twisted beliefs about right and wrong and human decency, allowed him to make decisions that caused death and destruction on a scale previously unknown. Likewise, the brutal dictator, the drug lord, and the warlord demonstrate a lack of respect for others and contribute to cultural deterioration as they pursue *power* (control). Unfortunately, just one such person in a leadership position can have a devastating impact on many others. Pictures of the atrocities and starving victims of warfare are appalling to those who promote a sense of universal human dignity. Why do "civilized" people allow their behaviors to be dominated by the desire for power or ethnic hatreds rooted in the distant past? Obviously, either they do not possess a sense of morality, their morality is selective, or it sometimes takes a back seat to more primitive forces. This occurs in relations between nations, ethnic groups, and divorcing parents in child custody battles.

This is not to imply that one who has a mature system of morals will never do anything self-destructive or harmful to others. Being the imperfect beings that we are, many on occasion do or say something that they later regret—something that was a "mistake" or "stupid." Most have even had the urge, however fleeting, to kill someone. Many have witnessed individuals lose self-control, become very angry or "go berserk," whether it was at the scene of a traffic accident or discovery of an unfaithful spouse. But, for most of us, destructive impulse behaviors are the exception. Why? We have internalized principles about how people *should* and *should not* behave and act accordingly. These principles act as constraints on impulses, and guide us in terms of what is right and what is wrong. And we lead "normal," socially compatible lives.

OUR PARADOXICAL BEHAVIORS

"Why in the world did he do that?"
"Does he know what he's doing?"
"That doesn't make any sense."

Commonly heard statements like these clearly reveal two things. First, we *need* to understand our surroundings. This requires integration of new experiences with previous learnings and established expectations. These expectations are based in part on previous learnings about what is "right" and what is "wrong." And second, we occasionally observe behaviors of others that are puzzling, that seem to contradict what we have learned to expect of those individuals because of previous observations. Sometimes when someone is asked why he did something, even he is at a loss to explain—like the child who responds with, "I don't know."

What accounts for these apparent contradictions? They can be explained in part by one aspect of human nature: We simply are not always consistent. For a variety of reasons, we on occasion do the unexpected, sometimes acting on impulse without really thinking about choices and likely consequences—and do something "out of character" or something that is a "mistake." Occasionally, our rational approach to tasks is overridden by strong emotions—which leads to more regrettable actions. Another factor that explains contradictory behaviors is the fact that priorities change occasionally as new experiences are integrated, as circumstances change, and as goals are accomplished and new ones are established. The process of maturation also accounts for some of the contradictions; as we mature physically, emotionally, and socially, as new experiences are integrated into our psyche, we view and value things somewhat differently. For example, how many times have we observed fundamental changes in people after a *life-shaping* experience—such as in soldiers after they had experienced combat firsthand, in our astronauts after walking on the moon, in people who survived a life-threatening illness, or in those who "settled down" after they got married or became parents? Of course, there is also the need for occasional change; we need routine in our lives, but too much becomes boring. How many times have we heard someone say, "Let's do something different?" Some erratic behavior can also be attributed to mental instability. But some erratic behaviors can undoubtedly be attributed to a lack of clearly defined moral values.

As complex beings, we also have a variety of seemingly contradictory needs and values. Consider, for example, the drug lord who expresses tender, loving feelings for his children. He needs and values close family relationships, but has no appreciation for the destruction he causes in other families. His value of wealth is a driving force. And herein lies a profound challenge: extending the individual's sense of belonging and morality beyond his immediate social circle to the society as a whole and even to the world. This can, of course, present a problem to the individual. For example, how does a scientist, who has a clear set of moral values, participate in the research and development of weapons designed to destroy human beings? This remained a troubling question for some of those American scientists who worked on development of the atomic bomb during the 1940s—even with their ability to justify it on the basis of national survival. And does a parent reveal to law enforcement officials that his son is trafficking in drugs? How about the gang member who will not "snitch" on a friend who committed an armed robbery or killed someone? These questions hint of the levels of moral development that were outlined by Kohlberg.

Differences in values and priorities usually also account for what appears to be confusing behaviors of others. How so? Aside from possible differences in maturity, each of us has a unique experimental background that begins in the family. And, as families differ, so too will the values and morals internalized by the individual.

Stages of Moral Maturity

In his approach to understanding moral development, Kohlberg described six stages of moral development, beginning with the *punishment-and-obedience orientation* and culminating with the *universal-ethical-principle orientation*.[3] Each succeeding stage represents decision-making based on a higher quality value. Devel-

---

[3] From Kohlberg, Lawrence, "From Is to Ought", In T. Mischel, *Cognitive Development and Epistemology*. New York: Academic Press, Inc., pp.164-165.

opment progresses from a limited orientation where *right* and *wrong* are related only to the immediate concrete situation to an orientation where broad ethical principles can be applied at all times and in all places. It also progresses from a totally self-centered and self-serving orientation to one that includes sincere care for the well-being and rights of all people. Kohlberg explained that a key element in determining an individual's stage of development is the reasoning he uses when he is confronted with conflicting moral choices.

At the beginning stage, *the punishment-and-obedience orientation*, right and wrong are determined by punishment consequences and by the power of the authority figure who makes the rules. If punishment follows an action, the action is wrong; if punishment does not follow an action, the action is right. Avoidance of punishment is the primary motivating factor. For example, the child decides to tell the truth solely because he knows that he will be punished if caught doing otherwise, or an individual pays his taxes solely because he fears the IRS will punish him if he doesn't. *Truth, duty,* and *fairness* cannot be comprehended at this stage.

In stage 2, *the instrumental-relativist orientation*, the individual decides right and wrong according to "what feels good" or what satisfies his needs. Action that satisfies his needs is *right*, and action that brings unpleasant results is *wrong*. The individual may occasionally help another person if it will help him satisfy a need. Elements of fairness, reciprocity, and equal sharing are present, then, but they are always interpreted in a physical, pragmatic way. They are a matter of prudence, not matters of loyalty, gratitude, or justice. For example, a child may let a friend ride his bicycle as a means of getting to play with his friend's remote-controlled car. Or an individual offers to let a neighbor use his lawn mower in return for using his neighbor's trimmer. Thinking typical of this level includes: "What's in it for me?" "What are the consequences?" "What is right and fair is what satisfies me." Lying and cutting in line, for example, are acceptable—as long as they help the individual get what he wants and he is not punished for doing so.

In stage 3, *the "good boy"/"nice girl" orientation,* the individual values and conforms to the expectations of others. What is right is what pleases others and wins their approval. A prime motivating force, then, is fear of disapproval. The individual strives for recognition from those whom he believes are important, such as his parents, teachers, and peers. For example, a worker decides to stay on after closing time because his supervisor will see him and praise him for doing so, or a child decides to help his mom do the dishes because she will like it. He also begins to judge behaviors by intention—if the person meant to do what was expected. If the child breaks a dish while helping his mom, he is not judged harshly because he was trying to help his mom.

Stage 4 is *the "law and order" orientation*. At this stage the individual is controlled by a desire to do what the social group or society defines as right and responds to the group. The individual respects authority, fixed rules, and maintenance of social order. *Right* behavior, then, is doing one's duty, showing respect for authority, and obeying rules/laws. At this level, the individual waits for the green light to change to red before crossing the street even when there are no approaching cars. An individual dresses a certain way to be like his peers, or because it is the way his gang has designated members to dress; fraternity members observe national rules of their organization; the soldier views "regulations" and discipline (adherence to "regs") essential to being a "good soldier." Concern for dishonor because of failure to adhere to the group code is high. At this level the individual is irritated, for example, when he sees a driver speed through a school zone, or someone cut in line at a checkout because these are violations of established rules of conduct.

In stage 5, *the social-contract/legalistic orientation*, right action tends to be defined in terms of general individual rights and standards which have been critically examined and agreed upon by the whole society, not by groups. There is an emphasis on established procedures for reaching consensus and, when necessary, on procedures for changing standards within the system. The result is an emphasis on the *legal point of view*, but with an emphasis on the possibility of changing law in terms of rational considerations of social utility rather than freezing it as in stage 4. Court systems and procedures for appeals and changing laws are basic components of this level.

Stage 6 is *the universal-ethical-principle orientation*. At this stage, individuals make decisions on the basis of universal ethical principles that are valid for all people in all places and times. Right and wrong are determined by the individual's conscience but within the framework of universal principles of justice, reciprocity, equality of human rights, and the dignity of humanity. The value of all life, compassion for fellow man, unconditional love, and respect for the rights of all people, then, are basic to this level. These universal principles transcend local rules and laws. They are broader in scope than the rules established by a social group and may be broader than the laws of a given society. The individual may refuse to obey a law if he believes the law to be unjust, that is, not in accordance with his beliefs about universal principles of justice. For example, the conscientious objector may refuse to serve in the military because he is opposed to war for any reason. Much of the apparent thinking in the U.S. Constitution and the American Declaration of Independence is on this level. This level of morality is likewise apparent in the Charter of the United Nations and in the World Court since they were established in part to be protectors of universal human rights and advocates of universal human dignity.

These stages, then, are also apparent in behaviors beyond the individual, such as corporate decisions and the nature of various institutions. For example, the military probably operates most efficiently with recruits who are no higher than stage 4. Why? Recruits on lower levels are more apt to follow orders without questioning them. The civil rights movement, as personified by Martin Luther King, Jr., represents stages 5 and 6. Responding to the starvation in Somalia in 1992 for purely humanitarian reasons, that is, caring for others as an act of love and recognition of universal human dignity, suggests stage 6. But creation of this situation in part by the superpowers who armed opposed sides during the Cold War suggests stage 2 of those respective governments; for the superpowers locked in a struggle for control of the Horn of Africa and important sea lanes, it was merely a matter of cold pragmatism.

As we examine the behaviors and rationale of others and ourselves, it becomes apparent that many of us never achieve the level of moral maturity described in stage 6—or, for some individuals, that described in stage 4 or 5. It seems today that more and more are operating on level 1 or level 2: it's okay if you "can get by with it" (don't get caught and punished)

Determining One's Stage of Moral Development

How do we determine an individual's level of moral maturity? Clues can be found in the individual's rationale or, more specifically, in his motivation or apparent reasons for decisions. For example, a thirteen-year-old who wants to have his hair cut a certain way because "everybody else is" suggests stage 4; one who changes his hair style because "they are making fun of me" suggests stage 3. A driver who observes speed limits only when a patrol car is in view because he fears getting speeding tickets indicates stage 1; one's conscientious observation of speed limits because he believes that everyone should obey the law, even when patrol cars are not in view, indicates stage 4. If an individual bases his decisions on the belief that "the end justifies the means," that any behavior is acceptable if it helps him attain his goal, he is either amoral or operating on stage 2. An example of stage 2 operation would be an individual's decision to stop a doctor from performing abortions by fatally shooting him. If it is a matter of prudence, a matter of the end justifying the means, then, the individual is likely operating on stage 2. An individual who is a vegetarian because he is afraid he would otherwise get cancer suggests stage 1; one who is a vegetarian because meats are too expensive suggests stage 2; one who is a vegetarian because he believes that it is wrong to kill other animals as a matter of principle, even though it is legal, suggests stage 6.

Complicating the determination of one's level of moral maturity is the fact, as implied earlier, that we sometimes operate at different levels. These fluctuations reinforce the need for multiple observations. They are usually prompted by changes in specific situations, such as who is watching, or conditions that allow emergence of more primitive emotional forces such as jealousy or anger. "Profound" experiences also may impact an individual's operational level, but on a more long-term basis. For example, an individual may be opposed to the death penalty as a matter of principle, but he may change his mind if a member of his immediate family is brutally murdered. One could argue, in such case, that the individual didn't really oppose the death penalty as a matter of principle in the first place, that he revealed his real belief when he was "put to the most severe test." But it is also widely recognized that such an experience and other "profound" experiences, such as winning a fifty million dollar lottery or surviving of a life-threatening auto accident, may have noticeable impact on an individual's values and morals. After all, we are, to a considerable extent, a composite of all our experiences. But, as noted earlier, these fluctuations or erratic behaviors also may result from other factors, including a lack of clearly defined moral values within the individual..

TODAY'S CHALLENGE

Every cultural group and society defines for itself what is appropriate behavior for its members. And, as noted earlier, it also establishes appropriate institutions and processes for teaching the young, social and legal controls for maintaining order, and penalties for those who deviate. These behavioral guidelines or expectations are the essence of morality in the group and are a significant part of the heritage passed on to each generation. Survival of a society, then, rests to a considerable extent on the transmission of its values and morality to each succeeding generation. As these beliefs and accepted norms change, society must change—for better or worse.

America has experienced significant change during the last two decades. Many are deeply disturbed by what they see. Some find little reason for hope in the future. Today we apparently face the proverbial "fork in the road." We have to decide if we are to continue deteriorating into a violent existence with little respect or concern for each other and where more individuals expect others to take care of them, or if America is to be a society composed of responsible individuals who care for and respect the rights of each other.

But before making this decision, we need a closer examination of what we *were* and what we *are*. Exactly how has America changed? What has been lost? What do we want to become? How we redefine ourselves as a people and address fundamental problems today will affect our future for decades.

Chapter III

A Changed America

In some respects, quality of life in America has deteriorated significantly in recent decades.

Given that a society's continued existence rests to a considerable extent on the transmission of its values and morals to each succeeding generation, how well has America done so during the past two or three decades? Aside from the material improvements and conveniences today, are we satisfied with today's quality of life and living conditions? Do we worry unduly about personal safety when out in public places? Or about the possible theft of our property? Are the electronic security systems in our cars, businesses, and houses really necessary? Should they be?

Few would disagree with the assertion that life in America has changed considerably during the past 30 years, even 15 years. We have improved models of countless products, such as *remote control* TVs and *desktop* computers, and many new products such as cellular phones and fax machines. Automobiles have better brakes, and factories are more efficient. Individuals have more leisure time and enjoy more recreational activities—even new ones like hang gliding, bungee jumping and "water parks." But the past two or three decades haven't brought changes only in products, leisure, and conveniences. *We* have changed also. And these changes in intangibles, such as our hopes, fears, beliefs, and values, play a significant role in the quality of life. Two such changes, for example, have been an increase in *fear* of being a victim of a crime, and the diminished role of the traditional family. Although change is unavoidable, many of today's living conditions were never imagined by those who grew up 30 or 40 years ago.

Change has been so dramatic that it's difficult for today's youth to comprehend many aspects of life in the "Fifties." During a recent casual conversation with a teenager about the frequent theft of autos and the various measures to prevent their being stolen, I mentioned that keys were usually left in the ignition in the small town where I grew up in the 1950s, and added that no cars were ever stolen. He looked at me incredulously. I noted that few bicycles were ever locked and that houses were usually locked only when families went on vacation. I couldn't recall any burglaries.

Like so many before, living into a sixth decade has afforded me the luxury of making observations about life and how it has changed since my youth. And like those others, I have on occasion been unable to resist the temptation of noting how some things were better "in the good old days"—and occasionally boring younger people with recollections. These changes apparently have impacted all segments of society, from individual relationships and families, to schools, churches, and politics. They have also impacted all ethnic and racial groups. Some changes have occurred slowly while others have marked dramatic shifts.

Of course there's the tendency to remember times past better than they really were, to see them through rose-colored glasses. Things weren't really all good during "the good old days." There was a "dark side" then as now. But even allowing for this tendency, it is easy to note many specific differences between life in the 1950s and life in the 1990s. And some of these differences mark a significant drop, in some respects, in the quality of life in America.

At the risk of boring those who remember, and causing the young to either question my credibility or dismiss it as irrelevant, I believe that it is necessary to consider some aspects of life in Small Town, America in the 1950s. The purpose of this look back is not to build a case for returning to the 1950s—because we can't. When one tries to "go back" by returning after a number of years to what was a meaningful place, one is nearly always surprised at how it has changed. What we don't realize is that, like places, *we* change. Each new meaningful experience not only marks the ever-fleeting present and affects how future experiences are interpreted, it also alters to some extent how we see our past.

Change is inevitable whether we like it or not—and it can be healthy. The purpose here is to examine life as it was and to identify those elements that are worth continuing or re-establishing as the case may be. More specifically, the purpose here is to identify those values and aspects of morality that "worked" in the Fifties and that appear to be worthwhile in tomorrow's world. This will by no means be a comprehensive comparison of all aspects of life of the Fifties with that of the Nineties; rather, it will focus on some of the more apparent elements that seem to be worthy of consideration.

AMERICA, CIRCA 1950S

It should first be noted that America, like much of the world, became much more urbanized during the last half of the 20th century as it's population grew by about 100 million. But it wasn't just an increase in population that brought about greater urbanization. While urban areas grew dramatically, the population in most rural areas declined sharply. Typically, farm families moved to town, and, as people began shopping for better prices and selections in larger nearby cities, business in small towns decreased and stores closed, leaving countless empty main street buildings. And with the decline of business in small towns, people began moving to cities for work. This change in itself makes re-establishment or continuation of some aspects of life difficult or impracticable. This abbreviated comparison will be facilitated by examining the following aspects of life in America: Social Control, Daily Living, Public Schools, The Family, Business Practices and Ethics, and Politics.

Social Control

In my class of about 100 students in the public school where I grew up in the Fifties, there were few changes from one year to the next. Occasionally, a new student arrived or moved away during the summer. We all knew each other and, as the first day of the next school year neared, wondered who would be in our classroom. I graduated from high school with most of my first-grade classmates. Many of us, then, were lifelong acquaintances—whether we liked each other or not.

This school/community stability was quite common in small towns across America during the 1950s. It provided a setting for development of lasting friendships and traditions in a community. Neighbors usually knew each other and "looked out" for each other's belongings when asked—whether it was watering the garden, "watching the kids," or feeding the cat. (This wasn't necessary very often, though, because mothers were usually at home, and people didn't travel often.) This contrasts sharply with the high mobility rate, lack of familiarity with neighbors, and the reluctance to "get involved" or come to the aid of others in today's urban areas.

The full-time mom and close-knit community atmosphere where nearly everyone knew each other were significant elements in social control. If an adult saw someone's child doing something that was unacceptable, the adult might very well express his disapproval to the child *and* inform the child's parents about it so appropriate action could be taken at home. Sometimes another kid might even "tell." And if a suspecting parent asked a child about something that had happened, the child usually told the truth because he knew that lying was "wrong" and that liars were usually "found out" and punished. Once a wrongdoer was found out, punishment, usually consisting of a strong admonition and restrictions or a spanking, was a virtual certainty. When combined with "the little voice" (conscience) that children developed as a result of church teachings, this atmosphere acted as a considerable constraint on children's anti-social behaviors. Children were quite aware of this and usually behaved in a prudent manner—either making sure there were no witnesses, using leverage against a potential "tattletale" ("...and I'll tell Momma that you..."), or "being good" in the first place.

Parents, then, expected children to "behave" because of community pressure to conform to what was considered acceptable behavior. Otherwise, parents of a child who, for example, was caught stealing were embarrassed and felt ashamed. Parents of a girl who got pregnant out of wedlock were likewise seriously embarrassed and shamed. Few girls got pregnant before marriage. This wasn't due to better birth control methods; it was a result of the fact that most students were not sexually active. And why were they not sexually active? There were several factors. Girls' fear of getting pregnant and mothers' admonitions about the wrongness of premarital sex were usually sufficient for girls to resist boys' advances. But there were even cases where a boy would "break off" a relationship because he feared that they would get "too serious." In cases of pregnancy, the girl typically dropped out of school, and the boy got a part-time job and continued his schooling. And, yes, the couple got married. Why? It was the boy's "duty" to take care of the expectant mother and be a father to the child. This seemed only natural since sexual intimacy normally occurred *after* an emotional bond was built during an extended relationship. Sexual intimacy, then, was viewed as a serious commitment between a couple. Multiple sexual partners and "no strings attached" sex were uncommon—especially for girls.

When teenagers displayed unacceptable behavior or committed a crime that required intervention by law enforcement officials— which was rare and, except for an occasional fight, not of a violent nature, the officials "turned them over" to their parents for punishment and disciplinary action. (This was even more likely if the child was from a prominent family.) Punishment and disciplinary action usually included an apology and restitution to the victim for any damages, a thorough reprimand, and sometimes restrictions and a spanking. This was nearly always sufficient because parents, fearing embarrassment in the community, felt considerable pressure to "straighten up" their children. It was rarely necessary to file charges, then—and this was done only after parents were unable to prevent repeated displays of unacceptable behavior. Law enforcement officials cooperated with parents as much as possible because they realized the importance of saving face in the community and the effectiveness of parental corrective measures.

Adults, of course, were also subject to social controls. For example, divorce seldom occurred because of the pressure on couples to remain married. (Only two of my classmates came from broken homes.) What were these pressures? Aside from a personal sense of failure, separation from children, loss of friends in a close-knit community, and fear of being alone, getting a divorce was a violation of a fundamental belief in the church and community: that divorce was morally wrong. There was a stigma attached to the divorcee. The divorcee was no longer allowed to participate in certain capacities in some churches and, in some cases, was even ousted from membership. The divorcee often became self-conscious of gossip—more often real than imagined. Couples in difficult marriages, then, usually elected to "work things out," in part because of the moral obligation, and in part because of the painful consequences of divorce. How about a couple just moving in together? This was considered to be immoral and was not an option. If a couple were "in love" and wished to live together, they were expected to make a public commitment to each other in marriage. Likewise, engaging in an extramarital affair was a serious social infraction. So was public drunkenness. Those who did so were also objects of gossip and social disapproval. Knowing one had to face one's disapproving neighbors each day was a powerful deterrent to these unacceptable behaviors.

When conflicts did occur between adults, as they naturally did occasionally, the individuals usually settled them directly and amicably. If a social conflict could not be resolved amicably, they simply avoided each other. If someone had been wronged in a business transaction, it was considered a lesson learned: Avoid doing business with that party in the future. (And word got around.) Few sought legal restitution when wronged. For example, lawsuits were the exception even in cases where individuals were injured in auto accidents that were the fault of other drivers. Why? Most people didn't believe in suing each other. They thought that people should work for any money they received. When someone did sue, unless it was a case that involved death or threatened financial ruin, an underlying stigma was attached to him. Some became distrustful of him. Lawsuits, then, were rare, and frivolous lawsuits were unheard of.

Daily Living

Downtown, small, locally-owned businesses lined main street. They included shoe stores, dress shops, barbershops, "five-and-dimes," drugstores, cafes, banks, grocery stores, even a department store. Strung out from the courthouse square toward the edge of town were filling stations, auto dealerships, and drive-in restaurants. Drive-in restaurants were, of course, favored hangouts of teenagers. And busy they were, especially on Saturdays when farm families drove in and shopped while many town residents were also shopping. Drivers often had to "circle the block" to find a parking space. Businesses depended nearly entirely on local patrons. Maintenance of a high level of integrity and friendliness with the local community, then, was essential to a business's future. "Word of mouth" advertising spread quickly and threatened any businessman who engaged in unfair or dishonest practices.

Saturdays were special. Farm mothers usually dropped their children off at the picture show, which was a real treat, then did the shopping for the next week. "Town" kids looked forward to playing with friends and cousins after helping around the house in the morning. Shortly after lunch, at least 150 children rode bicycles to the picture show. After crowding their bicycles in front of the theater and purchasing their nine-cent tickets, they settled in with friends to enjoy the double feature, serial, and cartoon—and refreshments.

Saturday afternoon movies were usually cowboy "shoot 'em ups." Occasionally there was a thriller such as *The Thing,* or a mystery movie like *The Third Man.* Violence was a part of what we saw—even in the cartoons. But it wasn't explicit; cowboys never bled. Their hats even stayed on as they "slugged it out." A common thread in the movies was a clear distinction between good and bad, with the good guys always winning, and the bad guys always getting killed or going to jail. This reinforced the theme in comic books, which were read by the hundreds, that crime didn't pay. When romance was included, the couple usually just rode into the sunset in cowboy movies. Sometimes there was a quick kiss on the cheek that embarrassed the sidekick. But nothing more. Even married couples, such as "Ozzie and Harriet" on TV, were not allowed to be seen in bed together; they had twin beds.

Parents didn't seem to worry about children's safety while at the picture show or while bicycling about town. They apparently trusted that their children would not be victims of foul play. But they still insisted on knowing where were, what they were doing, and whom they were associating. There were no gangs and, although a couple of boys occasionally got into a fight, no weapons of any type were ever a part of these fights. Injuries were nothing serious—a few scratches or skin abrasions, and an occasional bloody nose. But most of the time the only injury was a bruised ego. The most feared injury, however, was a torn shirt because it had to be explained to Mom.

By the time we entered high school, the Saturday afternoon matinee didn't have the appeal that it did earlier. Some boys began working in stores on Saturdays, and others helped around the house. Besides, with the new freedom that driving provided, teenagers willingly delayed recreational activities til evening.

Saturday nights for many teenagers meant "cruising" in cars with friends, wishing for a date with a dream, or going to a movie with a "date" until curfew—which was usually eleven or midnight. Sometimes after the movie, there was a quick stop at the hamburger drive-in for a soft drink and fries. Those who didn't have dates headed for the drive-in anyway because it was the main "hangout." Between brief stops at the drive-in for hamburgers, fries, cherry pies, and drinks, they rode around together, sometimes in one car, then in another. Occasionally someone would be challenged to a "drag" whereupon, the challenge accepted, the two proceeded out the highway where they would then "drag."

Sundays were usually quiet, slow days. Except for one or two filling stations, motels, and a cafe that opened late in the morning, businesses were closed. Many spent Sunday mornings in church, which was often followed by lunch with grandparents or friends. Some occasionally went on a picnic and spent Sunday afternoon at the nearby park on the Navidad River, playing with friends and cousins. Others went to their bayhouse at Port Alto. Some families visited relatives nearby. Children spent the day playing (we always found plenty to do) while parents played dominoes and talked. Town children of parents who owned farms often drove to the farm after lunch to hunt or fish.

After high school most of us departed for college or jobs away from our parents and hometown. And it wasn't until then that we first heard of marijuana or any other illegal drug. Drugs, then, simply were not a problem when growing up in Small Town, America during the Fifties. Only a few teens smoked cigarettes regularly or occasionally consumed alcoholic beverages. Why? Most considered smoking to be rather "trashy." Teenagers who did smoke were not class leaders. Smoking and consumption of alcoholic beverages were, however, more common among those who dropped out before graduation. But with the exodus for college and jobs during the 1960s, a few became consumers of previously forbidden products, especially beer. (Consumption of illegal drugs, most notably marijuana, didn't become popular until the latter half of the 1960s.)

As young people left Small Town America during the 1960s, business activity and community spirit didn't seem to be the same. Some communities even seemed to begin searching for a reason for being in various renewal activities, such as celebrations of local history, "bargain days" in local businesses, and parades. But America had already changed. As opportunities in rural communities diminished and the children of the Fifties followed those opportunities to cities in the Sixties, life as it had been known in small towns was lost.

There were poor people in my home town, quite a few of them. This was especially the case among minorities. We could tell by the way they dressed and how they talked. But they somehow "got along." People always seemed willing to hire someone who needed work—even when the employer had to "find something" for him to do. That is, they were willing to help others help themselves. Welfare, then, didn't exist as it does today. The strong work ethic and belief that the individual should be responsible for himself required him to work rather than just be given money. This is not to imply that charity didn't exist. It was available to families in emergencies from churches, individuals, and organizations such as the Lions Club, the Rotary, and the Knights of Columbus. But charity did not provide a way of life that continued from one generation to the next. The able-bodied were expected to work, to be responsible for themselves. As a matter of fact, many poor were too proud to accept charity. They *wanted* to work. This contrasts sharply with today's recipients of aid from federally-funded programs who continue generation after generation as a way of life, expecting society to be responsible *for* them.

If someone was arrested for a crime, which was rare, the wheels of justice seemed to operate faster than they do now. There weren't the seemingly endless delays and appeals of today. Those convicted and required to serve time, then, more willingly accepted the consequences of their wrongdoings and began doing so soon after their trial. Today, those convicted of crimes are either put on probation or serve time only after appeals have been exhausted—then serve an abbreviated sentence because of crowded prison conditions.

Few of us, then, worried much about security. There was no such thing as the steering wheel lock for cars, and electronic security systems were unheard of. As noted earlier, we didn't lock our bicycles, people normally left the key in the ignition of cars, and houses were seldom locked.

Public Schools

Today the media report regularly about problems in public schools, whether it is lack of achievement or shootings. Many blame these problems on a lack of discipline at school, inadequately trained teachers, or evidence of a need for more money. Teachers in many large high schools are afraid to venture into hallways, and security officers patrol the halls and school grounds. Teachers complain about students who don't want to learn, and parents fear their children will be innocent victims of gang-related violence. Most high school students use or have tried illegal drugs, and most are sexually active. In some high schools, birth control measures are dispensed, and day care is available for more and more unwed teenage mothers. And achievement test scores, which began a steady decline after a peak in the early 1960s, are lower today than they were in the late Fifties.

Some are baffled by the declining achievement test scores. They note that America is second only to Switzerland in spending for education. Teacher training programs have also been strengthened. Individuals who wish to become teachers are required to complete more college coursework. And instead of completing only an eight week student teaching program (as was common in the Fifties and Sixties), today's students are required to complete a full semester or school year of student teaching. (In some colleges this is called an "internship.") Experienced teachers are required to improve their preparedness for teaching: States and local schools commonly require them to complete workshops and/or courses each year. But despite increased spending and better trained teachers, student achievement continues to lag. Why?

The answer, I believe, lies largely in children's *lack of readiness for learning* when they come to school and in the school environment—which are reflections of society in general. Many children come to school with little sense of responsibility and self-discipline, and do not want to put forth the effort that learning usually requires. As discipline has deteriorated, social matters and survival have become more important than learning. And, unlike the Fifties when students who obstructed learning were the exception, students bent on disrupting classes are much more common today. Many teachers complain, "Students are getting worse every year." A good example of this deteriorated atmosphere was provided recently by a neighbor who was a high school teacher. When I asked her how things were going at school, she stated that the teachers were trying to train the students how to behave so they wouldn't "trash" the new high school they were scheduled to move into the next year. Training included "no food fights" in the new cafeteria. Apparently food fights were a problem in the old school.

Use of illegal drugs undoubtedly contributes to poor attitudes and the increase in discipline problems and violence on school campuses. But drugs are symptomatic of a deeper societal problem: a breakdown in the nuclear family and a decline in family supervision and support of children. A large percentage of students have experienced divorce of their parents. Some have been through two or even three divorces. And divorce, especially without professional counseling for both parents and children, is devastating to children. Some live in single-parent families where the parent is unable to provide close supervision and support because of work. Many children, as a result, simply are not being adequately trained by their parents in social matters, self-discipline, and responsibility.

Conditions in public schools in Small Town, America in the Fifties were quite different. Aside from one or two somewhat unruly students in a class, students generally came to school with an attitude that was more receptive to learning because their parents expected them to learn and "to show respect" for teachers. "Yes, sir," and "Yes, ma'am" were indicators of discipline common in classrooms, especially in the South. There wasn't such a thing as a "food fight." (Besides, our parents would have "killed" us if we had done such a thing because it was not only ill-mannered, it was wasteful. We were always told, "Clean your plate"—which meant eat everything on it.) If a child misbehaved at school, he was likely "in trouble" with his parents because he had embarrassed them. "You should have known better" was a common admonition across America.

As noted earlier, marijuana, heroin, and other illegal drugs were unheard of in schools in the Fifties. Smoking cigarettes and consuming alcoholic beverages were considered "low class" by most students. Disrespectful behavior was not tolerated. Yes, there were discipline problems, such as an occasional fight, which, significantly, never included use of weapons. But these were infrequent and often predictable—usually involving one or two relatively aggressive and undisciplined boys. Theft, which was considered a serious infraction, was also infrequent and, when it did occur, usually involved nothing more than a pencil or some other article. (Teachers made a big thing out of a missing pencil!) About 200 bicycles were parked in an open-access bicycle parking area and were not locked or stolen. This was apparently the result of the repeated admonition by parents and teachers, "If it's not yours, don't touch it," and certain embarrassment and punishment for doing so.

The Family

How it has changed! With exception of two of my 102 freshman classmates in 1955, my class came from intact homes—that is, from homes that included both biological parents. This was rather typical since divorce was taboo except in the worst of circumstances. This is not to say that every marriage, every home, was "happy" or mutually satisfying for each parent. Couples had problems then—as now. But couples seemed to take their commitment to each other, and to their children, more seriously and, when problems arose, usually "worked things out." This contrasts sharply with today's families. About half of all marriages end in divorce. Adding to the problem, over one-fourth of all American births are illegitimate—that is, born to single mothers.Among African Americans it is even worse: About two out of every three births are illegitimate. Apparently, many take the commitment to marriage rather lightly, while others seem afraid to make a commitment to marriage—preferring children without marriage or a "live in" arrangement first "to see if it will work." And where are the kids in all of this? Apparently, having children doesn't require much of a commitment!

The typical family of the Fifties provided clearly differentiated roles for men and women and fathers and mothers which, in turn, served as clear models for children. With specific responsibilities designated for each role, fathers and mothers generally accepted their responsibilities as prescribed by the community, leaving fewer areas for disagreement. Typically, the father was the breadwinner while the mother, as homemaker, did the housework and the shopping, and cared for the children during the day. Only a few mothers worked outside the home. (Significantly, this meant that, in most families, at least one parent was available most of the time to supervise children's activities.) Among farm families, the woman's role often was expanded out of necessity, including tasks such as feeding livestock and helping move farm equipment from one field to another. Girls typically helped their mothers with household tasks, while older boys were expected to do the lawn and help their fathers with other tasks. This is not to imply that boys were allowed to be irresponsible in the house; they too were expected to keep their rooms uncluttered and "not make a mess" in the house.

These role distinctions were reinforced as children grew up. Boys were supposed to grow up and "be something," such as a policeman, doctor, pilot, or fireman. (We were forever being asked, "What do you wanna be when you grow up?") While some girls expressed a desire to "be something" when they grew up, such as a nurse or a teacher, it was commonly understood that most would marry after high school or college and be homemakers like their mothers.

Bonding between parents and children was facilitated in part by a common belief that married couples were *supposed* to have children. It was also facilitated by the amount of time parents and children spent together. Mothers were at home most of the time, and families commonly spent mealtimes together. Children who lived near school often went home for lunch on school days, and fathers, when able, even came home from work for lunch. After school, at least one of the parents usually took time to check children's school papers and expected children to spend time doing "homework." This is not to imply that family life was all responsibilities and no recreation. Families enjoyed various recreational activities together. Fathers took sons hunting and fishing, mothers took daughters shopping, and families, often including grandparents, aunts and uncles, and cousins, occasionally went to stock shows, on picnics, and family "gatherings." As the Fifties progressed, more and more families began taking vacation trips and camping out. After many families became proud owners of TVs in the mid-Fifties, they spent considerable time together watching favorite programs such as "The Ed Sullivan Show," "The Hit Parade," "The Milton Berle Show," "Ozzie and Harriet," and, of course, "Father Knows Best." The point is, most families spent considerable time together and developed reasonably strong bonds.

Intact families, the belief that parents should look after their children, and mothers as homemakers facilitated close supervision of children. Children usually had to get their parents' permission when they wanted to do something away from the house. They had to be home by a certain time, and teenagers had to be home by curfew or a "reasonable hour"—which was usually nine o'clock on school nights and midnight on Fridays and Saturdays. Except for school or church-related activities, some teens were not allowed to be away from home after school. This enabled parents to be reasonably well informed about what their children were doing, and when they would be home.

This close family environment facilitated the transmission of values and morals from parents to children. Models were clear, and parents were unequivocal about what was *right* and what was *wrong*. Typically, parents were consistent, and values and behavioral expectations were reinforced in a variety of ways. These were, of course, reflected in children's "manners," which included, among other things, respect for elders. Manners were reinforced at school.

This contrasts sharply with today's nightly TV reminder to parents, "It's ten o'clock. Do you know where your children are?" The implications are that today's children may be away from the house any night at ten and that parents may not know where they are. Even worse, the assumption is that today's parents have to be *reminded* to think about the well-being of their children. Unfortunately, it does seem that children are supervised less today—in part because both parents are working and, in part, by the fact that so many children come from single-parent families where the parent must work. The inflation of the 1970s contributed significantly to this development since prices of so many products quickly doubled (or more) and a second income became a necessity. It's no wonder that "latchkey kids" began to appear in significant numbers during the Seventies. They remain common today.

Even worse, it seems that some of today's parents are too tired or too concerned with other matters to think about their children. This results in less supervision, especially when coupled with the more relaxed, permissive attitude of many parents. Sadly, in more and more cases, raising children is falling on the shoulders of grandparents.[4] Today about 3.2 million American children are being raised by grandparents—which is an increase of 40% in just the last decade! By race, about one out of every 25 white children and one of every eight African American children are being raised by grandparents. In addition, the art of parenting apparently has been lost to many parents. So we offer parenting classes at community colleges and at public schools at night. But this may be similar to attendance at the school PTA: Parents whose children are already doing well in school are the ones who attend; parents whose children aren't doing well don't attend.

In all fairness to today's parents, though, it is much more difficult to raise children in today's world than it was in the Fifties. This is especially the case for the single parent who also has to be the breadwinner. But even in intact families, both parents often have to work today just "to make ends meet." (Although many women went to work in factories during World War II and some continued to work in the Fifties, it wasn't until the surging inflation and divorce rate of the 1970s that many moms were forced to go to work.) Many moms work today as a result of the changed attitude about the role of women in society. Parenting is also more difficult today because America is a more open, complex society. Children are exposed to different value systems, and they are bombarded with street language and explicit sex and violence in movies and TV programs as never before. Further complicating matters, drugs are present in virtually all large high schools and in many middle schools, and gangs compete with many parents for control of children.

In the Fifties, the family played the primary role in helping children develop a sense of responsibility. Parents provided role models by being responsible for themselves and their children. Parents, in turn, expected their children to be responsible. Children typically had to "pitch in" around the house, helping with lawn care and weekly cleaning. Those whose parents owned farms also were expected to help with "chores." Many children were provided a weekly monetary "allowance" in return for work and were expected to manage their weekly finances. Children also were taught to set goals and work toward those goals; they established desired purchases as goals and saved their money until they had enough to purchase what they wanted. Even recreational activities were used as leverage to teach

---

[4] Linda L. Creighton, "Silent Saviors," *U.S. News & World Report* 111 (December 16, 1991) pp.80-89.

children a sense of responsibility. Children were often told, "Not until you..." For example, after families become proud owners of TVs in the mid-Fifties, children often were not allowed to watch TV until they had done their homework. (Getting to watch a favorite TV program was a reward.) Responsibilities came first!

This contrasts sharply with most of today's children. I didn't realize how much until I returned to the public schools as a classroom teacher in the early 1980s. One of the most surprising changes was the amount of jewelry, expensive clothing, and money that even middle class children had. Many of today's children have their own telephone (with private line), television, stereo, games and costly toys in their rooms. And many don't have to work for these items; they are provided by their parents. For many parents, this is the easy way out: It's easier to give in and let the children have what they want rather than "fight with them." For some, especially divorced parents, providing gifts and money for children is a matter of status and reduces their guilt about the divorce.

Well, what about the parental instinct? Don't adults just *know* how to raise children? Unlike many animals, we don't really have a parental instinct—that is, an instinct that enables us to automatically know how to raise children. What many believe to be a parental instinct is actually just the sex drive: Sexually mature adults, desire to engage in sexual intercourse. But knowing how to *raise* children is *learned*. Unfortunately, more and more parents are ill-prepared for this life task today.

Business Practices & Ethics

One of the most striking characteristics of business in the Fifties was the personal touch and trust that people practiced in business transactions. People didn't have personalized checkbooks. When someone wanted to write a check at the local grocery or other business, he merely flipped through the stack of checkbooks available at the checkout to find the one he needed, then wrote a check. No ID was ever required because everyone was on a first name basis. But checks from out-of-town strangers were generally also accepted without ID. People just trusted each other until there was reason to believe otherwise. They never "took a number" as they waited for service either. Why? With exception of a few businesses like Western Auto, most businesses were "mom and pop stores;" that is, they were locally owned, single-outlet businesses. The owner of the business was nearly always present in the store. In larger towns, of course, one could find a Sears and Roebuck or a J.C. Penney. But the late Fifties saw two developments that were to have a devastating impact on businesses in small towns: the shopping mall in cities and improved highways and freeways that made them more accessible to shoppers from surrounding towns.

More and more shopping centers began to appear in cities in the 1960s, and people from surrounding communities began doing more and more shopping in these centers. This movement to shopping centers accelerated as the 1960s progressed and soon encompassed many different shopping needs—from eating and entertainment, to automotive needs, apparel, and household items. Large retail chains became plentiful, and the personal touch of the "mom-and-pop" store was largely lost. Clerks and store managers in chain stores were just employees who served large numbers of people—and patrons began "taking numbers."

This move to large retail chains and shopping centers contributed to a basic loss of trust in the individual. Customers nowadays have to be "approved" for credit and provide an ID (or two) when paying with a *personalized* check. They even have to pay beforehand at the gas station. Of course, merchants have good reasons for this lack of trust: Too many people have driven off without paying, and too many "hot" checks have been written!

The attitude about method of paying for items has also changed. In the 1950s most people operated on a "pay-as-you-go" basis. Except for large purchases like a house or car, or farmers who sought bank loans to put in their next crop, people usually paid cash rather than "charge it." The prevailing attitude was: If something can't be paid in full, do without it until you've saved enough money to pay for it. Few, then, had credit cards. Those who did usually only had a credit card from a major oil company. Today nearly everyone has at least one credit card out of necessity. Car rental companies, for example, won't rent a vehicle to someone who doesn't have a credit card. Businesses and associations continue to bombard the masses with "pre-approved" credit card applications.

There also has been a change in service. For example, when a car pulled into a filling station in the 1950s, two or three attendants quickly came out, with one asking, "Fill her up?" another raising the hood to check the radiator and oil, and another cleaning the windshield and checking the air in the tires. Today, except at a few "full service" pumps, there are no attendants. And the pumps are usually turned off. Customers have to go up to the window and give the attendant the money for the gas they wish to purchase, who then turns on the gas pump—so the customer can pump the gas.

Another aspect to this change in service is *dependability*—or lack of it. In the 1950s, for example, when a repairman said he would be at a house at a particular time, he was there as promised. "His word is his bond" was a well understood and appreciated expression. This contrasts sharply with today's service and dependability—especially in the housing industry. For example, when new homeowners need a repair or service, they call the appropriate "sub." A date and time are usually arranged for the serviceman to do the work. As often as not, however, he not only doesn't "show up," he doesn't even call to tell the homeowner that he will need to reschedule because of some unanticipated development. So they sit and wait—wasting time and still in need of the repair. This blends well with the expression, "We'll get back to you"—which really means they won't.

Then there's the matter of profit. Somewhere along the line America moved from "a reasonable profit" to "as much as the traffic will bear." During the high inflation of the late 1970s, for example, jewelry stores were quick to raise prices for jewelry, citing the increasing costs of gold and silver. But when gold and silver prices plummeted in the early 1980s, the reduction of jewelry prices lagged far behind. This was recently reinforced when I shopped for a water softener from a major manufacturer. I encountered a wide range of prices for identical models from retailers marketing that name brand. How does this happen? Local store owners informed me that the manufacturer simply wholesales the water softeners to them. No suggested retail prices are offered. Retailers, then, instead of pricing the various models down from the suggested retail as necessary to promote sales, work from the wholesale price up. Each local retailer decides what to charge for each model. How does the retailer decide how much to charge? I was told by different retailers that prices are determined by the affluence of the local community—what the local population is able and willing to pay. And as communities vary, so do retail prices—sometimes by hundreds of dollars for identical models. Instead of marketing for a reasonable profit somewhere between wholesale costs and suggested retail prices, then, they typically charge whatever the traffic will bear. How about shopping around for the lowest price? If I buy one from an out-of-town retailer, my local store owner will not install it or service it. So much for shopping around—at least for that brand.

Of course there have always been price gougers and ripoff artists. As the consummate con man P.T. Barnum noted long ago, "There's a sucker born every minute." But this attitude became more common with the high inflation of the late 1970s when a widespread greed seemed to emerge—whether it was rapidly increasing prices by businessmen or demands by organized labor for wage increases that exceeded inflation rates and increases in productivity. The expectation of a *reasonable* profit largely disappeared.

Politics

Corruption in politics has been present since governments were formed and groups of people began competing for control of the public purse. Each generation thinks that society is "going to hell in a handbasket" and that politicians are leading the way. Indeed, much of Will Rogers's career focused on corruption in politics. Today is no different: Comedians keep us up to date on the daily shenanigans of today's politicians.

But, as illustrated by the movement to limit the terms of members of Congress, people today do seem to be more concerned with the failure of elected officials to address seriously the real problems confronting America. They argue that many members of Congress seem to be more concerned with continuing their careers, raising their salaries, and expanding their perks. They point out that, in addition to each House member's annual salary of $133,600 in 1991, each was allowed to spend up to $537,480 on his staff. And in 1992 each representative's allowance for office expenses was raised to $122,500. In addition, each was provided a franking account—which amounted to an average of $178,000 per member in 1991. Meanwhile, the rapidly expanding national debt continues to erode the hopes and the economic base of future generations—and who cares?

What accounts for the failure of the federal government to address the real problems confronting America? More than anything else, spiraling campaign costs and the desire to be re-elected. For example, in 1992, Congressional candidates spent a total of $678 million campaigning for office, an increase of 52% over 1990. As pointed out during the 1992 presidential election, these spiraling costs require the typical member of Congress to begin raising thousands of dollars per week, beginning the week he takes office. Such costs make him vulnerable to the interests of those who make "generous" contributions to his re-election campaign fund. Unfortunately, this is an opportunity for those with the deepest pockets.

But the needs of special interest groups, such as the tobacco industry, often do not coincide with the best interests of society in general. What's the upshot? Instead of focusing on the people who elected them and serving their needs, these officials are unduly responsive to the needs of these special interest groups. Otherwise, why, for example, would we continue to subsidize tobacco farming when it is well known that smoking is a serious health risk that costs our economy even more in health care costs? If we really want to do something about our national debt and health care costs—two *real* issues, why don't we stop supporting the tobacco industry (to the tune of about $40 million annually), prohibit the advertisement of tobacco products, and, instead, levy more taxes on them? Tobacco farmers have had enough time—since the surgeon general's report in 1964—to educate themselves and shift to farming other crops.

Apparently the first priority of many in government is re-election, which makes attending to the needs of generous contributors very important. Those who do so seem to have forgotten one of the fundamental concepts taught in high school civics classes: government *of* the people, *by* the people, and *for* the people. Elected officials are *supposed* to serve the people. Unfortunately, generous contributions have become a pervasive factor in the daily decisions of many members of Congress. When combined with the temptations attached to various perks, the basic integrity of a Congressman can be compromised. This was most clearly visible in the abuses of the Congressional Post Office privileges and check writing scandal in the House of Representatives. It continues to be apparent in the perks and lucrative retirement benefits that Congressmen enjoy—even when they serve as little as six years in office.

In fairness to members of Congress, however, much of the blame for the failure to trim the national debt ultimately lies with us. We demand that local Congressmen secure federally-financed projects, keep local federal installations operating, and continue federal purchases of locally produced products simply because they provide local jobs—even when such outlays are not in the national interest or are no longer necessary. Hence, we have the infamous "pork barrel"—expenditures that are essentially a waste.

But there is hope! We, the people, still have a basic sense of right and wrong and can rise to the occasion to demand that government do the right thing.(This was clearly demonstrated in the uproar over the Zoe Baird nomination for Attorney General. We *can* make a difference.) One of our first priorities should focus on re-establishing the financial soundness of our America. This will entail regaining control of federal spending and implementation of a plan to reduce the national debt. Otherwise, if deficits continue and the national debt continues to increase, our economic system and way of life will collapse. This will be a certainty if we reach the point where we can't raise enough taxes to pay the interest on the national debt. Re-establishment of fiscal responsibility will entail, among other things, addressing the pork barrel problem—efforts of special interest groups that selfishly serve a few even when it is not in the best interest of the country.

Political and campaign reforms, then, are clearly in order. Advocates of term limitations cite the 90%+ re-election rate of incumbents and point out that this contrasts sharply with historical precedent. Indeed, it does. Not surprisingly, this change coincides with the sharp increase in campaign costs and need for fund raising that have occurred *since* the 1950s.

THE DARK SIDE OF THE FIFTIES

The Fifties certainly weren't a bed of roses. One of the most glaring differences between the Fifties and the Nineties was brought about by the Civil Rights Movement of the 1960s. Prior to the mid-Sixties, America was an apartheid society—one divided into two different worlds, one white and one black. And despite the continuing discrimination today, the world of the Fifties for blacks was indeed much different. Freedom and economic opportunities were very limited. Jobs were largely non-skilled manual and menial labor. Travel also was difficult since they were generally limited to black-owned hotels, motels, and restaurants. In much of the country, their children attended poorly funded, segregated schools.

For fear of injecting a stereotyped bias that was prevalent in the Fifties, my judgments about black society must be guarded and limited. But I do remember some specific observations that might be somewhat enlightening. My early years on the farm where my father employed fathers of black families who also lived on the farm allowed me to have considerable contact with children of those families. Indeed, we played together nearly every day; in the summer we swam together in the canal every afternoon. We were friends on the farm. And like us, they went to town on Saturdays. When my brother, sister, and I were dropped off at the picture show, we sat in the main part of the theater; our black friends had to enter through a different door and sit in a small part of the balcony reserved for "colored." Blacks were expected to "know their place," and show respect toward whites by being rather subdued in their presence and "mind their manners." Poverty was widespread in the black community. But families seemed more stable, and usually included both parents—whether they were, as rumored, "common law" or not.

Other minorities, most notably Mexican-American where I grew up, also had fewer opportunities in the Fifties. Although Mexican-American students attended the school I attended, many dropped out after the seventh or eighth grade. This seemed especially the case for girls in the male-dominated Mexican-American culture because they were expected to marry and have families. Girls didn't *need* to go to high school. We did, however, seem to get along. Indeed, one of the brightest and most respected leaders in my high school class was a Mexican-American. But we did not date each other. And the school curriculum, like that for the blacks, provided no real attention to or appreciation of contributions made by Mexican-Americans.

Another characteristic of society in the Fifties that many would fault today was the restricted role of women or, more specifically, limited opportunities outside the home. In cases where women were allowed to work alongside men, women were often paid at a lower scale. For example, elementary school teachers (who were predominately women), were sometimes paid at a lower scale than secondary level teachers where more men were employed. Women also were limited to certain types of jobs. Administrative and managerial jobs were nearly always filled by men. Many professions were either closed to women, or women were allowed only a limited presence. For example, while there were many women nurses, very few were medical doctors. Few were lawyers either. And while most bank tellers were women, bank officers were nearly always men. Many low-paying jobs, such as clerking in five-and-dimes, drugstores, and department stores; waiting tables in cafes; and working checkouts in grocery stores were almost exclusively filled by women.

Women who remained homemakers, which comprised a large majority, were totally dependent upon their husbands for financial support. This made them vulnerable to an abusive spouse. In some homes where the husband was the breadwinner, the wife had little say in important decisions involving money. This made it impossible for these women to establish a credit rating—and even made it difficult for women who worked outside the home to establish a credit rating.

Lack of provision in schools for children with special needs was another shortcoming of the Fifties. Children who were mentally retarded or seriously emotionally disturbed, for example, seldom attended public schools. The few who did were usually enrolled in the regular classroom, which did not meet their needs, and dropped out during elementary grades. Most children who had special needs, then, either stayed home or were sent to a "state institution" away from home.

Some might also argue that the stronger social controls of the Fifties placed too many restrictions on individual behaviors, that there was not enough freedom. Obviously, a tradeoff between the freedom of the individual and social compatibility has to be made in each society. In the Fifties, greater emphasis was placed on social compatibility than it is today. Whether this emphasis is desirable is a matter of opinion. Today individuals seem subject to fewer social constraints. In some cases, social controls have diminished greatly or shifted. For example, as parental control has weakened, peer controls seem to have assumed a greater role in the lives of today's teens. As a matter of fact, gang members are typically recruited from homes where family ties and parental supervision are weak. For the typical gang member, then, the gang *is* his family.

QUALITIES LOST OR CLEARLY DIMINISHED

First, a further look at the Nineties. Have behavioral standards changed! What is often acceptable now would have been unthinkable in the Fifties. Today premarital sex, divorce, "live-ins," and illegitimate childbirths are much more common and apparently acceptable to a large segment of society. Sometimes it even seems that there are no standards! Some apparently believe that what is acceptable, what is *right*, is whatever they can get by with. For example, a 126 member marching band of an American university that was in Japan to perform during half-time ceremonies at an NCAA game in Tokyo in December, 1992 turned a shopping spree in an area noted for its electronics shops into a shoplifting spree—to the tune of $22,000. Another example was provided by tree thieves that same year. So many evergreens were being cut and stolen for Christmas from a university campus that university officials decided to start spraying them with a foul smelling odor as a deterrent. Some Christmas spirit!

According to the U.S. Department of Justice, one out of every four American families was victimized by violent crime in 1992. A report issued by the National Research Council in 1992 noted that

America leads the industrialized nations of the world in murders, sexual assaults, and other attacks, and concluded that crime "has degraded American life, left people afraid to walk their neighborhoods at night, put children in danger in school, and caused many to barricade themselves behind locked doors." (As if we didn't already know this!) A revealing example of our violent times was provided by an elementary school district in California in early 1993. So many of the district's students were being killed in cross fire that the school board was faced with the grim decision of deciding whether or not to buy life insurance for its pupils to cover funeral expenses!

Most worrisome, however, is the apparent adjustment (decision to live with) to higher levels of crime and violence, divorce, premarital sex, and live-ins as *normal*—"just the way things are." What is normal today, however, was not normal yesterday. Many even argue for legalization (normalization) of drugs that are clearly destructive. Divorce as the norm was characterized in a father's casual attitude toward family breakup when he introduced his new son-in-law to a friend with, "This is my daughter's first husband." And though we complain about crime, some of the biggest box office movies are riddled with graphic violence. Many parents have also adjusted to new norms. This is apparent, for example, in the common parental justification of birth control pills for their teenage daughters, "They're going to 'do it' anyway, so we better make sure they've got protection." It's also apparent in the parental surrender, "I decided to go ahead and let him go/do it/have it so he'll shut up." Apparently many parents simply can't muster the strength to say *no* and stick to it when it's in the best interest of their children. What they don't realize, however, is that children *need* limitations. What's the upshot of all of this? We are facing a social, educational, and moral meltdown in America today!

What, then, has been lost? The following have either been lost or now play a clearly diminished role in society.

— *A sense of security and safety in everyday living*, whether at home, while shopping, in parking lots, in schools, and neighborhoods—virtually everywhere. For many, their circle of trusted friends and acquaintances has become smaller and smaller as their fears of being victimized have grown and they have withdrawn behind barred windows and doors. This has resulted in a proliferation of security companies and security systems. We have installed security systems in our homes, cars, and businesses, and security guards patrol mall parking lots, parking garages, and schools. And school campuses aren't just "closed" today; many are surrounded with security fences like prisons with entrances that are locked during the school day. Security cameras monitor activities everywhere.

— *Personal integrity* has diminished. This includes not only a decrease in basic honesty, but also a less serious attitude toward commitments in business and in personal affairs.

— *Work ethic, pride in workmanship* has diminished. Today, about one out of ten people, most of whom are able-bodied, are on public assistance. Yet jobs go wanting. The common expression, "If you want something done right, you'd better do it yourself," reveals that pride in workmanship often leaves much to be desired.

— *A sense of personal responsibility.* Many parents fail to teach their children a sense of responsibility, generation after generation on welfare has become a way of life for more and more, and "passing the buck" is commonplace. School dropouts who are poor believe that they are entitled to benefits and a quality of life beyond that which their education and ability to work will provide, that they shouldn't be required to carry expensive car insurance, and that their needs for housing, food, and health care, for example, should be provided in part by others. They believe, in essence, that others should be responsible for the consequences of their own poor decisions, such as dropping out of school, using drugs, and having children that they cannot provide for. Property owners are usually found liable for injuries of individuals even when the injured party's behavior may have caused or been a contributing factor. For example, if a poacher falls out of a tree and injures himself, the property owner is liable. Or if one poacher accidentally shoots another poacher, the property owner is liable. (Laws, designed by lawyers, focus on the property owner who has something of value! And, of course, lawyers are one of the major beneficiaries of such tort laws.) Likewise, if someone drowns in a swimming pool after climbing over a fence (without permission), the owner of the pool is responsible. Lawsuits literally drove the small aircraft industry out of business in the 1970s because aircraft manufacturers, rather than pilots, were nearly always found responsible for crashes—even when pilot error obviously caused or contributed to the crash. Smokers who develop lung cancer sue tobacco companies even though the dangers of smoking have

The Challenge of the New Millennium

been widely publicized since the Surgeon General's report of 1964. In criminal trials, more and more defendants tearfully claim that their violent acts are the result of physical abuse by the victim or the result of drugs and/or lyrics of rock music. And juries seem to be accepting this argument more and more often! (It's as if the victim *needed* killing.)

— *Making and keeping commitments.* Commitments in business and personal affairs are taken much more lightly today. "No strings attached" premarital sex is common, nearly half of all marriages end in divorce, and lawsuits in the business world abound. Many just don't seem to worry much about keeping their word to others.

— *A preference for settling differences directly and amicably* without resorting to legal recourse has diminished. Knowing companies often settle out of court just to avoid costly legal fees, individuals today are quicker to file a lawsuit. Suing is viewed by many as "easy money." The bumper sticker, "Sue the bastard," said it all.

— *The ability to establish and work toward long-term goals.* Many individuals, especially young people, want things *NOW*! They find gratification of immediate needs and desires irresistible, and they seem unwilling to make necessary short-term sacrifices for long-term goals. Most tragically, young people without intermediate and long-term goals often seem adrift, as if they are waiting for a psychic or ouija board to bring them good fortune.

— *Respect for property of others.* Theft, as verified by the billions of dollars spent on security, is rampant and getting worse. The idea for many today seems to be: If you want it, take it.

— *Respect and caring for others.* The insecurities, lack of trust, and fear of lawsuits have led to an upsurge in avoidance behaviors. The lack of common courtesies and manners underlines the lack of respect for others.

— *Strong moral values.* There is apparently less emphasis on teaching children a sense of right and wrong. Many are not only lacking in common courtesies, they also are lacking in moral values that are indigenous to character development in a democratic society. As pleasure seekers, many value what makes them "feel good" at the moment. Others live according to ancient rules of power, aggression, and "don't get caught." Today there are fewer things that individuals will refuse to do as a matter of principle.

— *Family cohesiveness.* Nearly half of all marriages end in divorce, often leaving children in difficult situations. Each year about one million children watch their parents divorce.[5] It has become fashionable in some circles, even politically correct, as Dan Quayle learned, to glorify single-parent families. However, classroom teachers across the nation seconded Quayle's assertions about family values because they see first hand the greater difficulties children of divorce have emotionally, socially, and academically. Also, as today's children grow up and begin lives of their own, they are more likely to live away from their parents and see each other less often.

— *Parents who care about their children.* Apparently, many parents do not provide good models for their children, and they provide little or no training in basic skills, habits, and social amenities. They set few restrictions for their children and provide little supervision. The failure of many men to commit themselves to being fathers, divorce, and the sharply rising number of grandparents who are raising children are all indicators of a lack of parental care for children.

— *Safe schools for our children.* Violent crime in our schools, often children's use of deadly force against other children, has risen sharply in the last decade.

— *Children who go to school ready to learn.* As children's attitudes have deteriorated, so has achievement, which has declined steadily since the early 1960s.

— *Safe public parks and playgrounds.* Many are no longer safe, especially at night.

— *Safe roadside parks and rest areas.* People have ample reason to be "on guard" when they stop at one of these areas today. In many areas, it is inadvisable to use roadside parks and rest areas at night.

— *Traditional institutions/agents for transmitting values and morals to children*, such as the family, church, and school, play a less influential role today. In addition, today's popular literature and movies often entertain through graphic violence, aggression and passionate sex rather than emphasize the triumph of right over wrong.

— *Elected officials who view public office as an opportunity to serve* rather than as an opportunity for personal financial gain, and who

---

[5] Mortimer B. Zuckerman, editor-in-chief. "The Crisis of the Kids," *U.S. News & World Report* 114 (April 12, 1993), p.72.

implement fiscal policies that contribute to the fiscal and moral soundness of America.
— *A sense of community, of oneness with others in society.* As individualism and looking out for "number one" moved to the forefront and combined with a high rate of mobility, the sense of community and trust of those outside our immediate circle clearly diminished.

These losses, no doubt, are clear indices of a resurgence of *the beast within*—our self-serving, sometimes aggressive and violent instincts. As social controls have relaxed and the nurturing close-knit community and traditional family have diminished in importance, many have turned to other social groups (including gangs) and drugs for refuge and support. Surely, we can, we must do better.

WHERE TO FROM HERE?

We can't wave a magic wand and make all marriages happy marriages, make single-parent families go away, and make children grow up to be achievers and assets to society. Ditto crime, political corruption, racial tensions, drug abuse, and AIDS. It's going to take a well thought-out, *long-range effort* on our part. There are no quick fixes. And this doesn't mean just hiring tens of thousands of additional law enforcement officials and going on a prison-building spree. Why? Well, more of both are apparently needed in the short run, but hiring more and more law enforcement officials and building more and more prisons won't *solve* our problems; they only deal with the symptoms of deeper, underlying problems. The *causes* of problems have to be addressed.

The task at hand apparently requires two different efforts. The first, which will have more immediate impact, must deal with the seemingly "lost generation"—those adults and older teens who, for a variety of reasons, never went through the normal socialization process and who are unable to function within the parameters of what society has defined as socially and legally acceptable behavior. This effort must emphasize protection of society from such individuals, especially from violent offenders, more than the rights of those individuals. This means rehabilitation, long-term incarceration, or execution of repeat violent offenders. Unfortunately, the record of rehabilitation doesn't hold much promise.

The second effort must focus on today's young children and future generations. It requires consideration of what we are doing and what we haven't been doing in terms of (1) family life and parenting practices, (2) development of character and moral values in schools and homes, and (3) public policies and programs that support those institutions. This will necessitate programs and policies that promote fundamental changes in direction, and a determined effort on the part of parents and communities to deal with the tasks. Why? Without fundamental change, further deterioration of the family and its essential role in preparing children to be socially fit beings seems inevitable, violence will continue to grow, and society as we know it may disintegrate, possibly even degenerate into anarchy as individuals and groups increasingly resort to violence against each other. This won't happen in America? Don't bet on it. Daily life for many in our inner cities is already a nightmare! I realize this sounds alarmist, but the media provide more reasons every day to be alarmed!

We have to wake up. Many have become acclimated to the higher level of crime and fear of being victimized—as if they are normal. But normalcy is a matter of what is accepted and allowed to be institutionalized as a part of society. The growing drive for material possessions and pleasure has led us to neglect a core element of all enduring, cohesive societies: respect and caring for one another as individuals. Yes, we are generous in our charities. But I'm not referring to financial contributions—which are also convenient tax write-offs. I'm referring to *caring* for one another, our community, nation, and world.

How do we bring this about? In part, through renewed efforts in schools and homes to inculcate moral values in children as a vital part of their development, sensitivity training programs for older children who lack the abilities to empathize and other qualities important to social and cultural compatibility, and public policies that support these efforts. Suggestions regarding the family and parenting are offered in Chapter IV. In Chapter V, suggestions are offered regarding schools, with particular attention to helping children develop moral values. Chapter VI describes changes in public policies and programs that are essential to success.

Chapter IV

Toward Survival Of The Family & Good Parenting

*Parents are a child's first and most influential teachers about life—
for better or worse.*

There has been a growing concern during the past two decades about the state of the family and the quality of parenting in America. The *family* and *family values* have even figured prominently in the recent presidential elections. They continue to be major concerns today. These concerns, I believe, have resulted to a considerable extent from two perceived societal changes: a growing indifference of people toward one another and increasing crime rates. How are these related to the family? Critics claim that the breakdown of the traditional family and its failure to teach children socially compatible values and a sense of morality are contributing factors. The traditional family, that is, one that includes both parents and their biological children, clearly plays a diminished role in society today. Many assert that it has "gone to pot." They believe that most of today's societal problems would not exist if the traditional family had continued its prominent role in upbringing the next generation as it did during the Fifties. I agree to an extent, but other factors have probably also contributed to today's conditions.

Children raised in intact families tend to have fewer emotional problems and achieve more in school than children from broken homes. Why? Divorce is, in itself, a traumatic experience for a child even under the best circumstances. Children from divorced families tend to have more adjustment problems, more self-identity problems, and lower self-esteem. Why? Because of the turmoil leading up to the divorce, the divorce itself, which fills a child's world with uncertainties, because children often hear their custodial parent worry about her own adjustment problems and needs, such as paying the bills, and because they often receive less guidance and supervision when their custodial parent has to go to work. This is not to imply that children are *always* better off in intact families. Occasionally, conditions in intact families are such that divorce is clearly the better option.

We also need to remember that there are no guarantees in raising children. We cannot assume that all children from intact families will be well-behaved and do well in school. Neither can we assume that all children from broken homes and single parent homes are destined to do poorly in school and have insurmountable problems later in life. There are countless exceptions. Why? Conscientious, caring parents are found in all types of families, just as are child neglect and child abuse. The point is, although the intact family is an important factor, the *quality* of parenting is crucial—regardless of the type of family. Caring parents, whether they are divorced or not, who are interested in their children's development and who provide conscientious guidance and supervision are the most important environmental factor in shaping a child's development.

Still, the importance of the biological link between parent and child cannot be dismissed. Parents in intact families have a built-in reason to care for their children: The biological link provides a basis for bonding that begins even before birth, and a lasting sense of fulfillment in continuing the family name and traditions. It also can be a basis for greater embarrassment to parents. Misbehaving biological children present a greater threat to family heritage, tradition, and reputation than adopted children. Why? Unlike the adoptive parent, there is no "out" that allows them to blame it on someone else's genes. Obviously, then, biological parents naturally have significant reasons for supervising and guiding *their* children's behavioral development.

THE FAMILY

Development of the Family

The first social group formed by our earliest ancestors undoubtedly was the family. This was born out of some simple facts. First, like nearly all other living organisms, they were typed according to sex—male and female. Reproduction required sexually mature males and females to copulate. As they came into contact to satisfy their sexual need, behavioral patterns evolved to govern those encounters. Males and females behaved toward each other in certain ways. Males had to signal their virility, and females had to signal their receptiveness.

This was the beginning of role differentiation according to sex and, of course, the basis for heterosexual relationships today.

A second major factor further spurred *socialization* and development of the family: At birth, the young were totally dependent upon the adult for survival. This dependency continued for an extended period—considerably longer than in nearly all other species. Like members of many species, they quickly discovered that the newborn's chances of survival were significantly enhanced when *both* parents helped provide for its various needs. When coupled with the emotional identification with the offspring, the rather demanding long-term care required of the newborn made a cooperative relationship between the reproductive adults advantageous. This provided additional impetus for development of the *family*.

Formation of extended families or clans in which members were biologically linked was inevitable. This, of course, resulted from the realization that larger groups could more effectively protect themselves from predators and achieve a higher success rate when hunting. As social groups grew in size, their understandings about how they were to interact were expanded. This required refinement of role differentiation as well as awareness of what was not acceptable behavior within the enlarged group. Development of the concept of *fairness* and a *sense of right and wrong* followed.

Tomorrow's Family Needs

The first order today seems to be to provide services that are designed to keep traditional families intact. These support services should include parenting programs that focus on common problems such as dealing with sibling rivalry, helping the child develop a sense of identity, helping the older child establish a sense of independence, helping children develop a sense of responsibility, helping children develop values and a sense of morality that are socially and culturally compatible, establishing routine in the family, and providing a home environment that is supportive of school. They should also provide marriage counseling services that focus on problems such as maintaining a loving relationship in marriage, win-win conflict resolution in marriage, maintaining self-identity within marriage, and setting up and maintaining a family budget. Family counseling services also need to focus on problems such as parent-child conflict, planning for children's post-high school education, drug abuse (including alcoholism), and adjusting to remarriage and stepchildren.

If *all* children's chances of achieving a fulfilling, socially compatible life are to be enhanced, society must also deal with reality as it often exists today and provide supportive services for parents in nontraditional families. This means helping parents become able to provide for themselves and their children by providing training and education programs. It also means that society should take measures to ensure that the divorced parent who is legally directed to provide financial support for his children do so. It means providing child care for children of single parents whenever they are working or receiving job training. These efforts also should provide parent training programs that focus on common parenting problems and problems that tend to be unique to single parent families.

Tomorrow's Challenge: Good Parenting

As described in Chapter I, each newborn child brings within it a heritage of ancient instincts that developed in our primitive ancestors as a matter of survival. Some of the more noteworthy instincts are *aggression, spiritualism, power (control), reproduction,* and *territorialism.* Left unchecked, some of these instincts, can be socially destructive in modern societies that place a premium on acceptance of common rules of behavior and working together for the common good. The continuing hatreds, violence, strong drive for territory, and seeking of revenge in the world are examples of the emergence of these instincts (our "dark side") at their worst and their destructive power on society. They also are the source of sibling rivalries and children's fights.

Although they are defined differently in each society, these concepts continue to be some of the basic components in today's modern societies. One of the basic purposes of all societies, then, is to restrain and channel the energies of *the beast within* in acceptable ways. And in every society the most important agent for instilling those restraints and directions within the child is the family. The quality of parenting, then, is most crucial in the process of helping the child internalize those values and behavioral controls that will enhance his ability to function in society in a socially compatible manner. A breakdown in the family's responsibility to teach children these rules and behavioral controls, then, ripples throughout society—and it is becoming more and more apparent today.

Today's Child

How well have parents in America been doing? Examination of the social changes, the alarming teenage suicide rate, the growing violent crimes of teens, unacceptable high use of drugs, and epidemic teenage pregnancy rate indicate a significant decline in the quality of parenting during the past 10 to 20 years. Comparison of today's children and their home environments with earlier generations, especially with those of the Fifties, reveals several significant differences.

— *Today's child* is more likely to have witnessed an act of violence and to be a victim of a violent act. He also, then, experiences greater fear of being victimized.

— *Today's child* is more likely to have experimented with drugs or to be a user of drugs or alcoholic beverages.

— *Today's child* is more likely to come from an unstable home environment because of the frequency of broken homes and single parent homes. He more likely has to cope with living with stepparents, stepbrothers and stepsisters, and half brothers and half sisters—the modern extended family.

— *Today's child* is exposed to more graphic violence, street language, and explicit sex by the entertainment industry.

— *Today's child* has less experience in dealing with responsibilities.

— *Today's child*, as a teenager, may hold a part-time job, but he may have no job experience if his parents provide him with what he wants. The student who holds a part-time job tends to have more problems with drugs and other delinquent behaviors, has poorer grades, and participates in fewer extracurricular activities at school.[6] The child who has no job experience may not learn that work is normal and a necessary part of life, that it is a fulfilling life experience in itself. He may consider work to be demeaning. He may grow up without developing work habits such as scheduling a job, being on time, arranging necessary tools and materials for a job beforehand, doing a job right, finishing a job (and on time), and establishing a routine for jobs that have to be repeated at regular intervals.

— *Today's child* is likely to focus on short-term goals and immediate gratification rather than long-term goals and deferred gratification. This is born out in the part-time jobs that teenagers seek and

---

[6] Amy Saltzman, "Mom, Dad, I Want a Job," *U.S. News & World Report* 114 (May 17, 1993) pp.68-72.

their reasons for seeking those jobs. Most see work only as a means of getting spending money for things that they want "now," such as a car, clothing, or recreation experiences. Although some say they work so they can save for a college education, it usually doesn't work out that way. Little money is saved for college—which is a long-term goal.

— *Today's child* is more fun-oriented, less likely to be task or responsibility-oriented. He wants to be entertained.
— *Today's child* has been taught fewer social courtesies by his parents.
— *Today's child* has more unsupervised time after school and on weekends.
— *Today's child* spends more time watching TV, playing video games, and listening to music videos, and less time in intellectual pursuits such as reading.
— *Today's child* is more impulsive, less likely to engage in reflective planning and pursuit of constructive goals.
— *Today's child* has more money and material possessions—which are freely provided by his parents. (And yet, at the same time, more and more children are growing up in poverty because of divorce and single-parent families.)
— *Today's child* has a limited sense of the value of money. Since he has limited or no job experience and is given money by his parents, he is often unable to relate a dollar to time on a job. When he lands his first part-time job during high school or college, he is discouraged when he discovers the time and work required for minimum wage.
— *Today's child* is more likely to have serious emotional and social problems. Coping with the modern version of the extended family, lack of supervision by his parents, exposure to different cultures and values, and sometimes conflicting expectations from parent and stepparent leave him without a clear sense of direction. (This was validated by surveys of teachers in 1940 and 1990 about the top problems in America's public schools. In 1940 they identified talking out of turn, chewing gum, making noise, running in the halls, cutting in line, dress code infractions, and littering. In 1990 they identified drug abuse, alcohol abuse, pregnancy, suicide, rape, robbery, and assault.)

The Challenge to Today's Parents

There's no doubt about it, raising children isn't easy. It never has been. But it's more difficult today than during the Fifties—for several reasons. Today's economic realities often require both parents to work, which results in less supervision of children. This makes children more vulnerable to temptations and influences of other forces. Peer influence in general, gangs, and drug abuse, as a result, play a more significant role in children's lives today than they did in the Fifties. (Gangs and drug abuse, then, are essentially parenting problems.) The entertainment industry also plays a greater role in children's lives today. Children watch more TV and see more movies. And, as noted above, what they often experience vicariously is a world that includes far more explicit sex, street language, and graphic violence. Problems arise when children act out what they see in movies because they believe what is depicted in movies is reality. The difficulty of raising children today is even greater for divorced and single parents. And not just because of limited time for supervision. Divorce, including the turmoil leading up to it, often creates long-term uncertainties, fears, and anxieties in children.

We can't wave a magic wand and make divorce go away, make drugs go away, make the modern extended family go away, and make single parenting go away! And we can't make parents stay home to supervise their children after school. Many *have* to work. Supervision of children, then, remains a challenge to today's parents as do teen pregnancy, substance abuse, and violence. The problem in today's world of working and divorced parents is finding the time to spend with the child. This problem is compounded by the divorced parent who feels guilty about not spending enough time with his child and tries to "make it up" through material gifts and permissiveness. This is sometimes further complicated by divorced parents who use the child as a pawn in their continuing battles. (Their marriage didn't work, so why should their divorce?) No wonder today's kids have more social and emotional problems!

We also need to remember that parenting in our species is more complex and difficult than in other species. There are several factors that contribute to this greater complexity. First, the newborn human is totally helpless and dependent upon the adult for care. Unlike many animals, we don't have survival instincts that are triggered at birth and reduce the dependency upon adult care. (The two most obvious instincts that are triggered at birth, suckling and crying, actually signal the newborn's *dependence* on others.) Second, unlike many other animals, this period of dependency and need for protection spans a relatively long period. And third, the life that parents have to prepare their children for is far more complex than that of other species. We have a variety of cultures, roles, and thousands of different job roles to contend with. Also, our modern societies and economies require a very high level of interdependence. This interdependence requires development of many social skills, development of a considerable knowledge base, and preparation for entry into what is often a rather complex job market.

Why We Decide to Be Parents

If parenting is so difficult in today's world, why do we even bother to have children? The truth is, many of us are here by accident—carelessness that resulted in unwanted pregnancies. But many of us are the result of a desire to have children. Why do we *decide* to have children? Parents often cite one or more of the following reasons.

— Ego satisfaction—part of rite of passage to manhood, womanhood (This is also apparent when the first child is a girl and the father insists on a "second try" so "I can have a son," or when the first is a boy and the mother wants to "try again" for a girl.)
— Acquire a sense of immortality.
— Continue the family name (Jr., etc.)
— Create heirs for an estate or business.
— Have someone to look after us in our old age.
— Demonstration as an ultimate act of love, bonding of a couple.
— Fulfill social expectations (friends, parents *expect* us to have children).
— Enjoy children, watching them grow, helping them develop.
— Fulfill cultural/religious teachings about purposes of life—what we are *supposed* to be (parents).
— Satisfy curiosity about biological creative abilities.
— Leverage for financial assistance from parents or government agency.
— Pressure a lover into marriage.
— An effort to keep a marriage together.
— Create a person who can help make a better world (Now this is stretching it!)

Obviously, some of these reasons are *wrong* reasons!

Learning to Parent

So a couple decide to have their first child. Upon arrival at home with the baby from the hospital, however, the new mother is often gripped with fear of not knowing what to do. But don't we have maternal and paternal instincts that "kick in" and enable us to care for a baby? Well, not exactly. While *wanting* to be a parent is a result of social and cultural forces and our sex drive is instinctual, *being* a parent is learned. We have to learn how to parent children. And where do we learn how to parent? From our parents and by trial and error (and too often by error). We typically learn a great deal with the first child because we are more conscientious, but by the third child much has been forgotten, or we are just too pressed for time to provide the attention that was given the first. This, of course, usually shows up later in the behaviors of the baby of the family.

As one of the two or three most important roles in life (For those who choose to be parents, is there anything more important than being a good parent?), it's amazing that we take such a casual attitude toward parenting. Those who want to drive a car are required to receive appropriate training and be licensed. This is understandable and reasonable. Ditto plumbers, dentists, realtors, and beauticians. And electricians and pest controllers. The list is endless!

There is, however, a major exception: *parenting*. Nothing is required of people who want to have a baby—even though raising a child is far more complex and surely as important as driving a vehicle or plumbing! Apparently, we either believe that everyone is born with a natural ability to parent, or we consider parenting to be a personal right that no one can question. Yet, save for those relatively few who voluntarily enroll in birthing classes and parenting classes, new parents usually stumble into parenthood trying to remember what their parents did and hoping for the best. They usually end up adopting the style and techniques of their parents—for better or worse. This explains why parents who abuse their children often were abused themselves as children.

In light of the complex nature of child rearing and the difficulties of raising children in today's world, it seems obvious that parents need all the help they can get. This is reinforced by the growing number of parents who, when faced with behavioral problems in their children, don't seem to know what to do. Who hasn't heard a mother of a young child say, "I can't do a thing with him," or, "I don't know what I'm going to do with her"? Are these the same parents who ask themselves when their older child gets into serious trouble, "Where did we go wrong?" This is further complicated by the *close proximity* principle: It is easier to observe and analyze relationships from a distance, that is, when we are not emotionally involved, than it is when we are emotionally a part of the relationship. Why? When we are so intimately involved with a child on a daily basis, it is easy to be unaware of what may really be happening. We often simply don't realize the *real* impact of our behaviors on our children. This explains, in part, why it is easier to see how parenting behaviors in other families cause or contribute to children's behavioral problems. Surely, all parents could benefit from *some* parent training!

PARENTING FOR SUCCESS

What parenting behaviors best enhance the chances of a child's well-adjusted, successful life? This, of course, depends on several factors, one of which is the parents' perception of their role as parents. Crucial in this perception is their commitment to the child. Parents first should recognize that choosing to be a parent obligates them to certain commitments to the child. These include:

— An emotional commitment
— Time commitment (doing for, doing with, thinking about)
— Financial and material commitments (which affect total budget, change priorities, and divert money from other endeavors)
— Lifestyle commitment (where you go, what you do, when you do—willingness to sacrifice other endeavors)

Parental understanding of the basic rights of the newborn is also important. At a minimum, the child has a right to be:

— Wanted by both parents
— Raised in a stable, affectionate, and caring home environment
— Satisfied in basic necessities of food, shelter, clothing, and love
— Protected
— Raised in an environment that nurtures and stimulates its creative, intellectual, emotional, and social development
— Taught the knowledge, skills, and work habits that will eventually enable it to take care of itself
— Taught values, a sense of right and wrong, and etiquette that enable it to function acceptably in its society

Basic Principles About Child Development & Parenting

Today books about parenting are widely available in bookstores, and countless parenting classes are being taught in community education programs in schools and on college campuses. What do they offer? Although there are different schools of thought about parenting, they generally promote many of the same basic understandings and practices. Some have been accepted for generations. Those that have stood the test of time include:

1. Parents who have a realistic understanding of the commitments necessary for raising children create a home environment that is more conducive to children's healthy emotional, social, and intellectual development.

2. The first five years of an individual's life are most important in establishing a lasting feeling of security and in personality development. It is also the time when many potential problems can be prevented by parents who (a) apply sound principles in raising their child, and (b) establish a warm, caring, and encouraging relationship with them. Physical contact such as touching and hugging, soft-spoken reassurances, reading to a young child, and a stable home environment are of utmost importance.

3. Children learn much by observing the behaviors of others, especially their parents. Parents, then, are a child's first and most important teachers about life. Children naturally tend to acquire the attitudes, values, and behavioral styles of their parents. This explains, for example, the higher incidence of smoking among children of parents who smoke. Parents should be aware of this tendency and provide consistent, clear models that will enable the child to develop a feeling of security and an ability to adjust well in a democratic, culturally and racially diverse society.

4. As children grow, they pass through predictable stages and events in their development, such as the "terrible twos," puberty, and growth of peer influence. They also experience common struggles, such as sibling rivalries and the need to establish their independence from their parents. Anticipating and dealing appropriately with these developments is an important ingredient in effective parenting.

One important aspect of development, often neglected, is human sexuality. When is it appropriate to address this topic? Parents should be ready to respond in a specific, candid manner whenever the child inquires about any aspect of human sexuality. (This doesn't mean delaying discussion about the menstrual cycle with girls until after they have had their first period. Girls need to be prepared ahead of time.) How much information should be provided? Enough to satisfy the child's curiosity at the time of his inquiry. Parents, then, will usually need to provide more information for their ten-year-old than for their five-year-old. It also means that parents, sooner or later, will likely need to address some aspects of human sexuality that have long been taboo in many homes and sex education programs. Masturbation is one of these. How should it be addressed? As a normal part of human sexuality, as an intimate activity done in private, and as an activity that helps the individual cope with tensions created by the sex drive.

5. Children of intact families that include both biological parents usually do better in school than those from single parent families or broken homes.

6. Children of families in which members have a mutual, collective obligation to each other, work together toward common goals, such as saving money for a vacation, and strive for cooperation and harmony within the family achieve more in school.

7. Children of parents who supervise their out-of-school activities do better in school. This entails keeping track of what their children are doing, saying *no* when appropriate, setting restrictions or limitations on what a child can and cannot do, and expecting the child to accept age-appropriate responsibilities.

8. Parents who have a sense of drive and achievement, who prefer work and independence to welfare and dependency, have children who achieve more in school.

9. Children of parents who have a zest for learning achieve more in school because they also develop a zest for learning. This is reflected in parental interest in various topics, and in their readings and discussions with their children about those interests. Parental reading to young children is especially important.

10. Parents who value education, who support the school and teachers, who structure their children's home learning environment, and who help with their children's homework have children who achieve more in school.

11. Parents who have high expectations of their children tend to have children who do well. (Those who don't expect much, don't get much.) This doesn't mean browbeating a child to do better. Rather, the challenge is to set high, yet *attainable* standards for a child, then maintain a reassuring acceptance of the child while encouraging him

to achieve. Stimulation of a child to achieve is best effected by the parent who (a) models a zest for life, (b) establishes a routine for study and practice, and (c) supports his child's efforts with encouragement and assistance when it is appropriate.

12. The time families spend doing constructive things *together* is very important. Seemingly trivial things, such as doing work around the house, having meals together on a routine basis, engaging in recreational activities, and planning family experiences are very important. A family council—with a rotating chairperson, meeting each week at an agreed-upon time and focusing on problems, tasks and "what we" need to do—can also contribute to better communication, family cohesiveness, and enhance children's problem-solving abilities. Parental respect for children's ideas and feelings are crucial during such meetings. The council, then, should not become a time for parental preaching to children or a gripe session.

13. Although children often are not aware of the reasons for their misbehaviors, their misbehaviors are usually directed by four goals. They either want to *get attention*, *get power* (control, independence), *get revenge*, or *be left alone*. Parents need to recognize and respond differently to children's misbehaviors, depending on the apparent reason for each misbehavior.

14. Punishment. This is a topic where differences among experts and among schools of thought are more apparent. Positions range from rejection of all forms of punishment, to strong support of physical punishment (spanking, caning, and even the death penalty).

If punishment *must* be used, it should be used judiciously and on a limited basis. Why? Despite its sometimes apparent short-term effectiveness, punishment can be destructive. It often builds resentment toward the adult and sometimes results in retaliatory behavior such as not eating, fighting with siblings or classmates, and refusing to do homework. Even worse, physical punishment teaches children that it is okay for a power-person to inflict physical pain. Punishment also promotes a negative outlook toward life because it encourages children to weigh the value of actions not in terms of their inherent goodness, but in terms of the likelihood and seriousness of punishment. It implies that right and wrong are determined solely by whether or not punishment is a consequence of a given act, which is a very limited, immature view—stage 1 in Kohlberg's stages of moral development. Despite its limited deterrent value, then, the bottom line is that punishment not only has limitations, it also has serious potential shortcomings.

Studies about adults who commit violent crimes support this position on punishment. How so? Among such individuals, fear of punishment obviously is *not* a deterrent to violence; otherwise, they would not commit such acts in the first place. Findings indicate, instead, that most violent crimes are the result of: (a) impulse behaviors that spring from anger or rage that overrides rational thought processes (emergence of *the beast within*), (b) desperation, such as a drug dependency, that causes them to disregard possible punishment, (c) hatred that becomes such a driving force that it eventually causes them to disregard possible punishment, and (d) a failure to internalize conventional values and morals, resulting in individuals who believe that victimizing others to get what they want is acceptable—whether it is carrying out an armed robbery or murdering a doctor who performs abortions. Seldom is there any consideration or expectation of punishment prior to commission of most violent crimes. (This is not to imply that those who commit serious crimes should not be imprisoned. On the contrary, society must protect itself from those who victimize others, especially on a repeated basis.)

Does this mean that fear of punishment does not play a role in our everyday behaviors? Of course not. It often does, as evidenced by the reaction of most drivers to slow down when they see a patrol car approaching—even when they aren't speeding. And fear of getting caught (and punished) probably deters some from cheating on their spouses, many from cheating on their taxes, and others from stealing from their employers. But a far more effective and desirable deterrent to misbehavior or crime is the individual's development of socially compatible values and a sense of right and wrong—or morality. This is supported by the fact that we adults normally go about our daily activities behaving in socially compatible ways, not out of fear of punishment, but because we believe it is *right*. We observe traffic lights even when there is no opposing traffic or a patrol car in sight—and are angered when another driver runs a light. We wait our turn at the checkout—and are annoyed when someone cuts in the line. We provide vast sums for tuition-free public schools so all children can have a better chance at a decent life—and are angered when someone doesn't pay his "fair share." We are loyal to our spouses, in part, because commitments are important—and angered upon learning that a friend's spouse is cheating. This is at least stage #4 in Kohlberg's stages of moral development

Despite its potential shortcomings, however, many parents resort to punishment and threats of punishment to control their children. Such tactics often do stop misbehavior—at least temporarily. But the real challenge is to understand children's motives for misbehavior and respond appropriately. Children, for example, typically "test" limits placed on them on a regular basis, often to see what they can get by with in their continuing quest for freedom and power. And parents usually punish them when they repeatedly violate a limitation. But children may have other motives when they deliberately violate a limitation, such as to get attention or to find out if their parents really care.

Whether punishment is to be carried out and the nature of any punishment, then, should be determined by the nature of the child's misbehavior and his apparent motive. For example, if the child's objective is to get attention, the best possible response may be to ignore the child's behavior or just walk out of the room—that is, not give the child the attention he desires and seeks through misbehavior. If a child continues to clutter his bedroom floor with his dirty clothes, a parent might pick them up and refuse to let the child wear them again until he agrees to put them where dirty clothes belong. If punishment is necessary, the adult needs to communicate clearly that the behavior is unacceptable and specify why it is unacceptable. If an admonition is not sufficient, "time out," imposition of restrictions, withdrawal of privileges, and restitution are much more attractive than physical punishment. Whatever the case, it is important to communicate to the child that it is his *behavior* that is unacceptable, not him. It is also better for parents to emphasize the positive—to recognize and express appreciation for desirable behaviors rather than punishment for misbehaviors.

15. Rewards, such as praise, treats, permission to do something, or a trophy, are used by many parents to reinforce desirable behaviors in children. The fact is, we all need some positive strokes and generally respond well when they are received, whether it is a raise in salary, a promotion, or special recognition at a ceremony. But like punishment, rewards, despite their short-term effectiveness, can be counterproductive. If rewards are dispensed too frequently, they become meaningless. In addition, they often become ends in themselves, especially with young children. That is, the child tends to lose sight of the value of the desired behavior the adult hopes he develops because he focuses on the valued reward instead. (We've all seen the first grader whose sole objective is to "please the teacher.") Parents,

instead, should show their children that they have confidence in them and support their development of desirable skills and habits with training time and necessary paraphernalia. They also need to focus on teaching their children the *inherent* value of the desired skill or habit. When criticism is necessary, it should be of a constructive nature. That is, the parent should calmly demonstrate again how to do the desired task. Criticism that is overdone or carried out in a heavy-handed, negative manner often leads to diminished self-respect, frustration, and rebellion.

16. Don't overreact to a child's mistakes. Parents should remember that they make mistakes—and that children are no different. When a child makes a mistake that needs attention, sitting down and talking calmly with the child will be more effective than yelling and "making a big deal" out of it—without instilling trauma in the child. Why? A calm, thoughtful reaction enables the child to focus on the mistake and needed corrective measures rather than the parent's anger. Parents, then, need to avoid acting on first impulse.

17. Take time to teach the child basic skills and habits. Don't wait until he does something wrong and react critically, telling him that "you should have known better." Anticipate the child's need to learn how to do something and show him how, then encourage him to try it, patiently assisting as needed. Then expect him to develop the habit of doing so.

18. Don't do for the child what he can do for himself. Begin teaching him a sense of responsibility early in life—"helping" Mom, "helping" Dad, picking up after himself, keeping his room uncluttered, and so on. This can be expanded to additional tasks as he becomes more capable, such as cleaning his room, helping with the laundry, working in the garden, and mowing the lawn. This will enhance the child's self-esteem and prepare him to take care of himself. If he is provided a reasonable weekly "allowance," don't give him more when he demands it—expect him to learn to live within his budget.

An important element in teaching a child to be responsible is allowing, even expecting, a child to take on responsibilities and develop worthwhile habits. Indeed, if a child is to become able to handle a responsibility, he must be given opportunities to learn how to do it. This, of course, carries with it the possibilities of failure and success. But even with failure comes learning, especially with proper supervision. Parents, then, have to be able to set aside their natural desire to protect their child and allow him to take the risks associated with learning to handle a responsibility. As the child feels his parents' confidence in him, his confidence in himself will grow.

Though practically all parents will say that they want their children to learn to take care of themselves, many parents handicap their children through misguided efforts to "help" them—either because they fear that their child will fail, or because they subconsciously want their child to continue to be dependent on them. Well-meaning parents who repeatedly "bail out" their children financially or legally often create a pattern in which they are forever helping their children—even into adulthood. Such help merely extends their children's dependence on them. What happens when this help continues into adulthood? The child never grows up, never becomes an independent, self-supporting adult. He remains a dependent, demanding child and the relationship based on financial and/or emotional dependency continues. A state of emotional incest may develop in these relationships in which the child, regardless of his age, is unable to think of himself as separate from his parents. Such children are forever children, unable to make decisions on their own and make a life for themselves away from their parents. The proverbial "apron string" is never cut. Rather than becoming responsible for themselves, their parents continue to be responsible for them.

Parents, especially mothers, then, need to be alert to their own need to be needed. When they find themselves constantly reminding their children and doing things for them, they are reinforcing a dependency relationship—which is ultimately destructive to the child. Such parents need to have other interests and give their children room to grow and become independent.

The problem is: knowing when to help and when not to help. When is it wise to help a child? When the help supports the child's development of basic skills and habits and his ability to take care of himself, including his pursuit of a career and his ultimate independence. Paying for a child's college education or treatment at a drug rehab center, then, is an investment in the child's future independence. When help reinforces the child's long-term dependence on his parents, it is destructive.

19. Don't give the child everything he wants or let him do everything he wants to do. Otherwise, he'll grow up thinking the world owes him a living, and he'll tend to act on impulse rather than contemplate options and consequences. Besides, children find limitations to be psychologically comforting, total freedom disconcert-

ing—even though they'll never say it. Parents should remember that humans have unlimited wants but must live in a budgetary reality. To give a child everything he wants or let him do whatever he wants is a terrible disservice to the child.

20. Knowing when to say *no* to a child is very important. As a rule, the parent should trust his first judgment after he has given his child's request some thought—and stick with it. It is appropriate to say *no* when:
— The child's action will place himself or others at unreasonable physical risk or undesirable social risk
— The child's action will infringe on the rights of others or place an unreasonable hardship on them
— The child's action will interfere with previous commitments to others
— The child's action will interfere with or prevent completion of a task already under way

Probably the worst thing a parent can do, even worse than always saying *yes*, is to first say *no*, then, after the child's whining, begging, temper tantrum or other negative behavior, give in and allow the child to do what he wants. Such action by a parent reinforces the negative behavior of the child. The parent unwittingly trains his child to throw temper tantrums, whine, or exhibit other undesirable behavior. How so? Children quickly learn behaviors that get them what they want—and they remember to behave likewise in the future when a parent says *no*. Parents always need to keep in mind, "If I do this, what am I teaching my child?"

When should parents begin saying *no*? It is important to begin teaching children very early that there are limits to what they can do and to what they can get. This means saying *no* when appropriate before the child is two years of age. Failure or delay in this can result in an older child that is both demanding and difficult to control. Parents need to remember that it is *much* easier to teach a young child about limits than it is to gain control of a fourteen-year-old.

21. When setting limits or restrictions for a child, parents should discuss their concerns with him and, when possible, allow him to help establish the limitations. This will help him understand what is expected, communicate that his opinion is valued, and help him develop a feeling of ownership in the system.

But remember, even after having some say in setting restrictions, children normally "test" them on a fairly regular basis. They do so to see if parents (or other authority figures) really mean what they say, to see if the parameters of what is acceptable can be expanded, and to get attention or power. (When the authority figure "gives in," they win.) Children typically "work on" the parent they believe more likely will allow them to do what they wish. If that parent says *no*, the other parent is approached. If a crack is detected in parental solidarity, it will be exploited. ("But Momma said I could!") Parents can avoid being outwitted in this manner by adhering to the established limitations and, when necessary, checking with the other parent.

As noted earlier, however, a key indicator of a child's maturity is his ability to assume new responsibilities and exercise new freedoms in a responsible manner. And a fundamental task in parenting is to teach the child to behave responsibly. As the child matures, then, restrictions are eliminated as he assumes new responsibilities and as new freedoms are granted. The challenge to the parent is to judge *when* a child is ready to assume a new responsibility or a new freedom. As the child assumes responsibilities, he gains his parents' trust which, in turn, allows them to grant new freedoms—one by one. This doesn't mean, however, that there will be no failures or disappointments. On the contrary, they will occur—and parents have to be ready to respond by reinstating a restriction or by providing additional teaching.

22. Parental denial and self-delusion about a child's wrongdoing often are contributing factors to children "who go wrong." Parents need to be realistic about their children, be honest with themselves, and accept the fact that no child is perfect, not even their own. They need to guard against emergence of their egos and protective instinct when a teacher, neighbor, or someone else communicates unfavorable information to them about their child's behavior. Indeed, there is a natural tendency for parents to react defensively to such reports because they are often interpreted as a criticism of the parents' parenting skills and a threat to the family's reputation. There is a natural tendency, then, for parents to react defensively to protect their children, their family reputation, and their self-respect. This tendency even prevents some parents from attending parenting classes because they view attendance as an admission of their inadequacy as parents. But emergence of this defensive mode, unfortunately, can prevent dealing with a problem early on when it is easier. A realistic outlook is that any child will occasionally make a "mistake," and, when presented with the possibility of punishment for wrongdoing, may first deny the event or omit details unfavorable to him when describing

the event. Yes, parent loyalty to a child is very important, but being realistic about the possibility of a child's misbehavior and expecting the child to admit to any wrongdoing and face reasonable consequences (restrictions, restitution to victim, frank discussions about the wrongness of the act, etc.) is not being disloyal to the child. It is teaching him an important lesson about values, actions, and consequences in life.

23. Having fun together is an essential part of a healthy family environment. Whether it is a favorite hobby, camping, or playing "one-on-one," participating in fun activities as a family and sharing individual experiences with each other help establish and maintain a friendly relationship.

How to Raise a Loser in Life

Conversely, if a parent wants to raise a child who is self-centered, uncaring, unable to take care of himself, and most likely to fail as an adult, just do the following:

1. Give the child everything he wants, let him do whatever he wishes whenever he wishes, but, of course, only after you have first said *no* and he has whined or thrown a temper tantrum.

2. Whenever he is accused of wrongdoing, always refuse to believe it; accuse others of picking on him and defend him at all costs.

3. Don't give him any responsibilities. Do everything for him. This way he'll expect the world owes him a living.

4. Don't worry about commitments to others. Whenever you or your child change your mind, that's okay.

5. Let him stay out at night as long as he wishes, and don't concern yourself with what he's doing. Trust that he's learning to take care of himself.

6. Fight with your spouse regularly, especially in the presence of your child. Then get a divorce and blame your child for the divorce.

7. Blame your child for everything.

8. Become a habitual abuser of alcohol, use illegal drugs, and refuse to practice common etiquette in your child's presence.

9. Complain regularly in your child's presence about how unfair the world is, how untrustworthy people are, how people who are racially or ethnically different are the cause of all problems.

The Challenge of the New Millennium

10. Never admit to your child that you are wrong, never apologize for a mistake.

11. Never take time to listen to your child or take his wishes into account.

12. Never tell your child that you love him. This way he'll be better prepared for a rough and tumble world, a "dog eat dog world" where only the strong survive.

13. Teach him that it's okay to do whatever he wants as long as he can get by with it (avoid getting caught).

14. Always compare him unfavorably with his brothers and sisters, telling him things like, "Why can't you be like your brother?" and, "Your sister wouldn't have done that," and show obvious favoritism toward his siblings, letting them do things he is not allowed to do, and giving them more than you give him.

15. Raise your child in a chaotic, unorganized home environment where there is little or no routine so his life will be filled with uncertainties and inconsistencies.

16. Physically or sexually abuse your child. This way he'll grow up hurt and angry, more likely to abuse others, especially his own children.

In summary, children who end up later as adults with emotional problems, a lack of constructive direction in life, and difficulties in leading socially-compatible lives are often the result of several parenting/home factors. Most common are:

1. Inadequate supervision by parents
2. No limits placed on child's behaviors by parents
3. Undesirable parent role model
4. Physical/emotional abuse or neglect of the child
5. Failure to teach a child a sense of self-responsibility
6. Failure to teach a child a sense of community (constructive identity with others)
7. Poor attendance and achievement at school (often becomes a school dropout)

Good children, then, don't happen by accident. They are the result of a persistent, conscientious effort by caring parents. Parents have to care enough to supervise their children adequately, to say *no* when appropriate, to insist that their children learn to do for themselves, to insist that their children stay in school, and so on. This is neither simple nor easy. But the reward of seeing one's child grow up and do well in the adult world makes it all worthwhile.

Chapter V

Schools For Tomorrow's Needs

Schools and parents must work together more closely to help children become constructive members of society.

Schools have traditionally borne major responsibility, second only to parents, for "molding" each generation into capable adults who are ready to assume the responsibilities of citizenship. Billions are spent annually on professional salaries, buildings and equipment, and teaching supplies and materials. When the children don't turn out right, it's no wonder, then, that some blame our schools. (It's called, "passing the buck.") Teacher training programs have been beefed up, experienced teachers are required to continue their education, and programs and materials continue to be updated. But student achievement, despite a slight recent improvement, remains significantly below what it was in the 1950s and early 1960s. What's wrong?

What critics fail to realize is that schools don't operate in a vacuum. They are, first, reflections of society as it exists. As noted in Chapter III, they are a part of society and, as such, are impacted by broader societal problems. And have schools changed! Today, concerned parents don't just worry about their children's learning while at school, they also worry about their safety because of the increasing violence and drug use on school campuses. Security officials patrol hallways and grounds, and, in some high schools, teachers are afraid to venture into hallways. How in the world are schools going to lead our children into the future?

Although various factors contribute to our societal problems, many of our problems, as noted in Chapter IV, can be attributed to shortcomings in family environment and parenting. Today we are all paying the costs of poorly educated single mothers, working parents who don't adequately supervise their children, and the "modern extended family" with all its parents, children, stepparents, stepchildren, and half-siblings. Today more children come to school with emotional problems, insecurities, little sense of personal responsibility, and little self-discipline—all of which significantly affect their *readiness for learning*. And herein lies much of the reason for the current state of our schools: There is no substitute for a stable, caring home environment.

Let's face it, schools, especially as they currently exist, simply cannot fill the vacuum left by deficient or dysfunctional home environments. And they can't, by themselves, solve society's problems. The best bet is a closer, coordinated effort by the home *and* school—as was originally intended. What we need to do is re-examine the purposes of schools and adapt them to current needs, with particular consideration of the shortcomings of the family and parenting. And since a child's most important teachers about life are his parents, these efforts obviously should include various parent support and parent education programs. There also needs to be a renewed emphasis in schools and homes on character development, including socially compatible values and a sense of right and wrong. These efforts should begin early in a child's life at home and continue through his school years with a coordinated effort at home and at school. Public policies should support and reinforce these efforts.

Otherwise, more and more adults and children will seem to be adrift, without a sense of direction or purpose in life. Indeed, the search for security and a surrogate home base lead some to gangs or to religious fanatics who take control of their minds and financial assets—sometimes, as we saw near Waco, Texas, with disastrous consequences. Others seem to be led along by four survival principles: *"Might (power) makes right," " It's okay if you can get by with it"* (don't get caught), *"If everybody else is doing it, it's okay,"* and *"If it pays the bills, it's okay."* Some morality!

Will a renewed effort on character development and moral values result in a moral straight jacket and less freedom for members of society? Not necessarily. It should, however, result in living conditions that are safer for individuals to enjoy their freedoms and achieve their aspirations. (Sadly, today our freedoms are being limited more and more by lawless individuals who victimize us as we go about our daily affairs, whether at home, school, work, shopping, or driving on the freeway.) We need to mobilize public opinion that "enough is enough," and implement programs in character development and moral values in schools and homes that will provide a solid foundation for life and help youngsters achieve their dreams and aspirations. Of course there will always be some anti-social, criminal elements in society. But implementation of programs designed to help children develop socially-appropriate moral values that have *universal* application is in serious need—and should result in citizens who are more likely to be assets to society.

But what moral values should be taught? To answer this question, we first need to consider what society normally requires members of each new generation to learn. Essentially, there are two basic tasks. Each new member is expected to:

1. Become able to interact with other members of that society in constructive, socially compatible ways, and
2. Grow to his full potential socially, intellectually, and culturally, and develop talents and skills that are emotionally rewarding and that enable him to provide for himself.

To achieve these goals, the individual normally internalizes certain values and rules that govern how individuals are to interact. These rules also act as constraints on natural behavioral tendencies (ancient instincts). Each society normally provides an environment and processes that enable its young to learn those values and rules (morals) so he can achieve those ends. The family, schools, and spiritual institutions have traditionally borne major responsibility for transmitting these matters to the young. In our society, they have focused on development of:

1. Personal responsibility (and accountability)
2. Personal integrity
3. Respect for public and privately-owned property
4. Acceptance of a work ethic that rewards individual initiative

Purposes of Our Schools

As noted above, schools have traditionally been charged with part of the responsibility for "molding" children into socially-compatible beings who are able to provide for themselves. But what does this entail? What must children *learn*? While there is some disagreement about the daily learning activities and learning materials used in our schools, most of us agree on those qualities that contribute to a successful, rewarding, and satisfying life of the individual. They include development of:

1. Values that are socially and culturally compatible
2. A sense of right and wrong that is socially and culturally compatible
3. A sense of purpose in life (short-term, intermediate, long-term goals that are based on socially and culturally compatible values)

4. Basic living skills in communicating, organizing, calculating, managing a budget, driving an automobile, and managing time
5. Occupational/professional job skills
6. A sense of cultural heritage and appreciation
7. A positive self-concept
8. Character traits that enable the individual to function effectively in a society, including poise, patience, a sense of humor, honesty, respect for others, compassion, punctuality, loyalty, open-mindedness, initiative, tactfulness, ingenuity, perseverance
9. An interest in and respect for our world
10. A sense of belonging and commitment to family, friends, society, and humanity, and an interest in playing a constructive role in social and civil affairs
11. A sense of responsibility for one's self and freedom to choose one's own destiny
12. Personal skills such as the ability to establish and maintain friendships, observation of appropriate etiquette, the ability to establish and maintain an intimate relationship with another person for purposes of meeting various personal needs, the ability to cope with loss, the ability to cope with change, and the ability to maintain personal hygiene and implement good health practices

Although these elements are listed as separate items, they are not isolated from one another. They are quite interrelated in the real world; development or failure to develop one will affect others.

Why are these elements important? They provide clear directions for setting up curricular goals in our schools, and they aid in the identification of those values that are important for the student to internalize. The values described later in this chapter are derived from these tasks. They are presented here as desirable goals even though it is apparent that many in our society today do not internalize these values. I believe that internalization of these values by an individual will significantly enhance his chances of achieving a successful, rewarding life at work and on a personal level, and will result in a richer society for all—regardless of his/her ethnic, racial, or religious heritage.

THE HIDDEN CURRICULUM

But hasn't the teaching of character and moral values in public schools been controversial? Yes, there has been considerable debate about the inclusion of values and morals education in public schools.

Those opposed to the inclusion of these matters in the curriculum have argued that values and morality should be taught only in the home and church, that they are too personal, too crucial to character development to entrust to public schools, that teachers might somehow "subvert" children if allowed to teach values and morals. This is nonsense. Values and morality have always been the hidden (and sometimes not so hidden) curriculum in schools. (Besides, we know full well that the typical home has clearly fallen short in this task.)

How so? As noted earlier, values and morals are powerful, unseen forces through which we filter all of our experiences. Everything that we say and do not only communicates some literal message, it also communicates something about our values and morality. We cannot escape them. They determine how we spend our money, how we spend our time, what we believe is right, and how we interpret and respond to behaviors of others. They shape our daily decisions, goals, and destiny. Even the fact that we have schools communicates something about our values. The nature and purposes of schools, then, are reflections of our values and what we think is *right* (and wrong). They are derived from philosophy—the study of the nature, purposes, and processes of life. What is taught, how it is taught, and the general school environment, then, are reflections of the prevailing philosophical concerns in a given society. This is especially the case in a democratic society where schools are ultimately controlled by the people: What schools are and what they are supposed to achieve are ultimately decided by the people. Values and morality, then, have always been a part of our schools. Some just haven't realized it.

But how has this hidden curriculum been taught? Aside from their academic progress, children are continually being appraised and provided feedback by teachers and principals about the acceptability of their behaviors, beliefs, and attitudes. In other words, how they *should* and *shouldn't* be. This feedback is communicated through:

1. "Deportment" and "citizenship" appraisals on report cards.
2. Praise/blame assertions by school personnel.
3. Non-verbal reinforcement (smiles, frowns, etc.) from school personnel.
4. Teachers' apparent values and morals as observed by students.
5. Discipline policies.
6. Dress codes.

The issue, then, isn't whether or not values, morals, and character are taught in schools; it is, rather, *what* should be taught and *how* it should be taught. We have to decide if we are to deal with these matters as an unseen undercurrent outside the usual school academic curriculum, as noted above, or teach them directly, that is, as a part of the planned program of instruction. With the diminished impact of the family and church on children's development of values and morals, on the one hand, and the soaring substance abuse, violence, teenage suicides, teenage pregnancies, and crime in general, on the other hand, the indirect, incidental approach at school is obviously inadequate for today's world. The role of the school in children's development of values and character must be expanded. Besides, many of today's parents hurriedly go about their daily affairs, trying to "pay the bills," with little or no thought about what values and morals they are teaching their children. Some don't seem to know *what* they believe. They provide inconsistent models for their children, in some cases, and provide little or no direction in others. The point is, values and morals are *not* being adequately attended to at home! Schools *have* to take a stronger role, not only emphasizing these matters at school, but also providing a sense of direction and programs for parents.

Is the public ready to accept this expanded role for schools? I think so. This is supported by the fact that the number of private schools increased by 30% during the 1980s while public schools decreased by 3%. (By 1991 5.3 million students were attending private schools.)[7] These parents frequently cite the poor learning environment and the lack of emphasis on values and character development in public schools as reasons for sending their children to private schools. These parents, who are taking on an additional financial burden, have given up on our public schools. They are now demanding that they be given tax credits; that is, that they be exempted from paying taxes that support public education. This is a sad testimonial to public education in America.

Admittedly, public education in America is afflicted with serious problems today. We read about them every day. Sometimes it seems that public schools are being blamed for all of our troubles. But we can't give up on them. They have provided a basis for America's leadership in the world in agriculture, medicine, science and technol-

---

[7] Thomas Toch, et al. "The Exodus," *U.S. News & World Report* 111 (December 9, 1991): pp.66-77.

ogy, business, and virtually all other fields of endeavor for generations. We have to remember, however, that schools are a reflection of society in general. And therein lies the challenge: Today America is confronted with serious societal problems that cannot be solved by schools alone. But schools, can, in a coordinated partnership with educated, conscientious parents, make a significant difference. There is no attractive alternative. Why not private education? Public rejection of voucher systems clearly indicates opposition to use of public funds for private schools. The question is, if public schools were converted to a private education system, who would pay the tuition and other costs of educating children from families who could not afford private education? Since it obviously wouldn't be in the public interest to leave them uneducated, *taxpayers* would have to step forward.

A Brief Review of Values & Morals in Our Schools

If children are to be taught moral values in schools, what should be taught, and how should it be accomplished. First, a review of what was have done in the past. Through the early 1960s, values and a sense of morality were transmitted to the next generation by a rather autocratic approach. Youngsters were, for the most part, told what to believe and were expected to behave accordingly. They were taught to respect those in leadership positions. Children were expected to internalize a clear set of beliefs, including, among other things, respect elders, authority figures, property of others, truthfulness, personal responsibility, good personal hygiene, patriotism, work, family togetherness, and God as the Creator of all things.

These values were reinforced in concert by the home, school, and church. If a youngster "got in trouble" at school, he dreaded going home and facing his parents because they were usually informed about "the problem" even before he got home. Parents seldom questioned the judgments and decisions of school personnel, and usually reinforced school punishment with punishment at home. Techniques most often employed to teach values and morals included clear-cut historical and fictional heroes who were always victorious in their struggles against evil in movies and comic books, models, admonitions, limitations of choices to those that were acceptable, appeals to conscience, use of value/moral-oriented school materials such as the McGuffey Readers, punishment for wrongdoing, threats, and regular teachings of the church. A question commonly asked by teachers after reading a story was, "What's the moral of the story?" The following story from the McGuffey Reader series illustrates the strong moralistic overtones of many materials used into the 1950s.

The Insolent Boy[8]

James Shelton was one of the most insolent boys in the village where he lived. He would rarely pass people in the street without being guilty of some sort of abuse.

If a person were well dressed, he would cry out, "Dandy!" If a person's clothes were dirty or torn, he would throw stones at him, and annoy him in every way.

One afternoon, just as the school was dismissed, a stranger passed through the village. His dress was plain and somewhat old, but neat and clean. He carried a cane in his hand, on the end of which was a bundle, and he wore a broad-brimmed hat.

No sooner did James see the stranger than he winked to his playmates, and said, "Now for some fun!" He then silently went toward the stranger from behind, and knocking off his hat, ran away.

The man turned and saw him, but James was out of hearing before he could speak. The stranger put on his hat and went on his way. Again James did approach; but this time, the man caught him by the arm and held him fast.

However, he contented himself with looking James a moment in the face, and then pushed him from him. No sooner did the naughty boy find himself free again, than he began to pelt the stranger with dirt and stones.

But he was much frightened when the "rowdy" as he foolishly called the man, was struck on the head by a brick, and badly hurt. All the boys now ran away, and James skulked across the fields to his home.

As he drew near the house, his sister Caroline came out to meet him, holding up a beautiful gold chain and some new books for him to see.

She told James, as fast as she could talk, that their uncle, who had been away for several years, had come home, and was now in the house; that he had brought beautiful presents for the whole family; that he had left his carriage at a tavern, a mile or two off, and walked on foot, so as to surprise his brother, their father.

She said, that while he was coming through the village, some wicked boys threw stones at him, and hit him just over the eye, and that mother had bound up the wound. "But what makes you look so pale?" asked Caroline, changing her tone.

The guilty boy told her that nothing was the matter with him; and running into the house, he went upstairs into his chamber. Soon after,

---

[8] *McGuffey's Third Eclectic Reader, rev ed.*, Eclectic Reader Series. American Book Company, 1920 (1879); pp.159-163.

he heard his father calling him to come down. Trembling from head to foot, he obeyed. When he reached the parlor door, he stood, fearing to enter.

His mother said, "James, why do you not come in? You are not usually so bashful. See this beautiful watch, which your uncle has brought for you."

What a sense of shame did James now feel! Little Caroline seized his arm, and pulled him into the room. But he hung down his head, and covered his face with his hands.

His uncle went up to him, and kindly taking away his hands, said, "James, will you not bid me welcome?" But quickly starting back, he cried, "Brother, this is not your son. It is the boy who so shamefully insulted me in the street!"

With surprise and grief did the good father and mother learn this. His uncle was ready to forgive him, and forget the injury. But his father would never permit James to have the gold watch, nor the beautiful books, which his uncle had brought him.

The rest of the children were loaded with presents. James was obliged to content himself with seeing them happy. He never forgot this lesson so long as he lived. It cured him entirely of his low and insolent manners.

The late 1960s saw the emergence of a new school of thought about teaching values and a sense of morality: *values clarification*. This approach was based on the premise that since America was such a diverse society, it was inappropriate for schools to attempt to impose a specific set of values (and, by extension, morals) on children who came from many different backgrounds, many different subcultures. This resulted, in part, from the realization that America really wasn't a "melting pot," that it was, instead, a complex society, and that it was becoming increasingly diverse. In addition, the Civil Rights movement and the Vietnam War protests contributed to the realization that blind allegiance to national leaders was not always or in the best interest of the people, that being a patriot didn't mean never questioning the word or judgment of national leaders.

In keeping with this philosophical basis, the main thrust of *values clarification,* although a direct, organized approach to teaching children values, was not promotion of a specific set of values. It focused, instead, on helping children clarify or become aware of their values through various "clarifying" activities. This approach was rather widely followed in schools that implemented instructional programs in values. By the early 1980s, however, the shortcomings of this approach had become more apparent. Critics charged that it simply helped children clarify their values—whatever they were. They argued that the process and activities did not require children to examine whether or not their values were self-destructive or consider their appropriateness in the broader cultural context. The apparent goal was simply to enable the individual to become aware of or clarify what he valued. And *whatever* he valued was acceptable. These concerns were undoubtedly a response to the rising anxieties about increasing crime rates, a growing general lack of respect for each other, a breakdown of the traditional family, and perhaps a desire for a time when values seemed clearer and more harmonious. The question is: What kind of program will most effectively help today's children internalize desirable moral values?

A Strategy for Teaching Children Moral Values

Young children, being the keen observers they are, normally "pick up" many mannerisms, expressions, and attitudes of their parents. This is most apparent in children's modeling or role play in which they "try out" roles of their parents and significant others, such as older siblings, friends, and teachers. Parents are often amused when they see themselves portrayed in their children's role play. Occasionally, they are even surprised when their children reveal something about them that they weren't really aware of—or hoped had gone unnoticed by their children. Indeed, role play is a significant component in children's learning process about life and living and, as such, plays an important part in their social development. When combined with parents' and teachers' overt efforts to teach them values and a sense of right and wrong through traditional techniques, such as admonitions, reasoning, rewards, and limitations on their behaviors, it is quite unlikely that a child will grow up without acquiring some values and some sense of right and wrong. This approach to teaching children values and a sense of morality, then, *does* work—at least it has to a reasonable degree for generations. When employed on a *consistent* basis at home and school, children do learn which behaviors are acceptable and which are not. Indeed, they learn early on "how to get along." However, the extent to which they *internalize* the desired values and develop a sense of morality depends to a considerable extent on the techniques employed, how the child is

The Challenge of the New Millennium

respected and loved, and how consistently and clearly the moral values are modeled.

How to Teach

Beginning in the 1960s and continuing today, critics of the traditional approach to teaching values and morality have argued that it is too authoritarian and will not work in today's world. Some have argued that simply telling children what to believe and how to act is grossly inadequate, that children need and deserve much more. I agree. But it should be noted that the traditional approach to teaching children values and a sense of morality is much more than simply admonishing or telling them what is important and how to behave. As noted in Chapter II, it also includes desirable role models, induction (reasoning, explaining consequences of choices), limitation of choices, rewards for desirable behaviors and punishments and non-responses for undesirable behaviors, as well as other techniques. It does not necessarily have to be carried out in a heavy-handed, authoritarian manner. Generations of parents who have employed this approach have provided children with thoughtful, considerate responses when their children asked, "Why not?" Many parents have recognized for years that raw power plays like, "Because I said so," do not win children's minds; they build children's resentment and "turn them off."

But are traditional techniques to teaching children values and a sense of morality enough in today's world? Probably not, especially since today's children are exposed to a greater range of value systems and influences than children of the Fifties were. Matters are further complicated by today's greater prevalence of broken homes, stepparents, single parent homes, and homes where both parents work full-time—which often leave children confused, without a clear sense of direction. And in schools, confusion about what values to teach in our diverse society and fear of lawsuits have caused some educators to de-emphasize values/morals/character education.

A strategy for teaching children values and morality in American schools today apparently should combine the best of the traditional approach with effective values clarifying activities. Indeed, it isn't possible to shut out the traditional approach. Children will always be keen observers of "significant others" in their lives, beginning with their parents, and be influenced by what those individuals believe and the behavioral models they provide—whether it is socially compatible or not. This strategy, then, should include traditional techniques, with emphasis on modeling a clear set of moral values, and induction (discussion and reasoning that focuses on choices and their consequences). It should also include appropriate values clarifying activities that are designed to help children sort out the values and components of a sense of morality that they can live with and that are socially compatible. For example, one value-clarifying activity that I developed and implemented with older students was the *Feelings Log*.

The Feelings Log was developed in response to the fact that adolescents are typically so strongly influenced by their peers that they often do not explore or develop feelings and opinions of their own. Rather, they go along with the prevailing opinions and decisions of peer leaders. The Log provides the student an opportunity to record and examine his feelings as related to specific actions of others. Its underlying purpose is to enable the student to develop or discover those principles that he believes *should* guide human interactions. It may also cause him to consider his own behaviors more critically and act more consistently. The activity is structured as follows.

The student makes entries in his log on a regular basis (each event or each week). Each entry consists of three parts which are arranged across the page. Multiple entries eventually result in three vertical columns on the page. The entry in the left column describes an action by someone that disappointed him, annoyed him, or made him angry. In the next column to the immediate right, the student writes how he *expected* the person (or persons) to behave in that situation. The entry in the right column focuses on a principle that he believes people should follow. Below is one of the examples that I provided my students.

| While jogging on a country road, some teenagers threw beer bottles at me as they drove by. | I expected them to drive by without incident, ignoring me—or, perhaps, wave as they passed by. | The safety and rights of others on roadways should be respected. |

Who should be responsible for teaching children values and morals? Aside from those first in charge—parents and schools—the influence of their peers can't be eliminated. Nor would that necessarily be desirable. For better or worse, as children enter adolescence, the influence of peers moves to the forefront. This need not be regarded as a threat to all the good that parents and other institutions have already accomplished. Children can be good influences on each other. The goal should be to help children begin to develop a socially compatible foundation of values and a sense of right and wrong *before* they reach adolescence.

As they enter adulthood and become aware of the responsibilities that accompany it, they often gain new respect for their parents. This was described so well by Mark Twain when he observed how much "the old man" (his father) had learned between the time when he (Mark) was a teen and when he became a young adult. What he was actually poking fun at was the transformation that older teens go through when they are exposed to the realities of the adult world. It's as if, "Wow, the old man knows more than I realized." Characters in popular literature and the broader entertainment industry should also reinforce those values and morals taught in the home and at school. Of course, this presents a problem in a democracy: freedom of expression verses censorship.

What to Teach

If values and morals are to be taught in public schools, *what* should be taught? Are there universals that are worthy of teaching to *all* children in our multifaceted, democratic society? There has been considerable debate about *which* moral values to teach children—and fear among some that teaching a specific set will put society in a moral straightjacket, quash the values of those cultural and ethnic minorities who differ somewhat, that in a multicultural society, such as America, there is no common ground in values and morality. I believe there is. Cross-cultural universals do exist. Furthermore, I believe that if an individual internalizes those universals, his chances of a life that is more fulfilling personally, socially, and, yes, even materially, will be enhanced. There's no need to worry about putting people in a moral straightjacket. Children can't be *forced* to internalize a given moral or value, no matter how attractive it might be. All society can do is set up learning conditions that promote these universals and hope they will be internalized.

The following moral values are proposed as the core curriculum for American school children and for values and morals programs designed for more mature participants. Although they are based, in part, on the examination of life in Small Town, America of the Fifties, I believe that they can serve equally well as a foundation for life in the 21st century.

1. *Honesty/truthfulness* (personal integrity) in dealing with others in their personal lives, business, and all other interactions; the individual displays personal integrity and a desire to follow through with commitments to others.
2. *Intact, loving family* (both parents and their biological children) viewed as the most desirable environment for propagation and child rearing.
3. *Self-reliance*, including goal-setting and management of necessary resources for achievement of those goals, providing for own basic needs and achieving recognition for doing so.
4. *Accountability for decisions*, not only enjoying the fruits of one's decisions, but also accepting any undesirable consequences without blaming others, and responding to undesirable consequences of decisions in a socially constructive manner (learns from mistakes).
5. *Respect for property of others—public and private.*
6. *Sensitivity to/respect for the dignity and rights of others*, and a desire to respond to the condition of those less fortunate in an understanding, helpful way when needed.
7. *Tolerance and respect for the right of each person to determine his/her own lifestyle.*
8. *Personal ambition*, the desire to become, achieve; to develop occupational/professional job skills and assume a socially and legally responsible job role that is sufficiently financially rewarding for the individual's desired lifestyle and property accumulation.
9. Other character traits such as *self-control, poise, patience, compassion, a sense of humor, a sense of purpose, punctuality, loyalty, open-mindedness, tactfulness,* and *initiative.*
10. *Development and maintenance of a mutually satisfying, intimate relationship* with another person for the purposes of meeting the need for companionship and satisfaction of emotional, social, and sexual needs.
11. *Development and maintenance of friendships* for the purpose of meeting various social and emotional needs
12. *Work as the preferred means for meeting financial needs* for living and acquiring property, and for achieving financial independence; that work is good for the individual physically and emotionally, and that it makes a constructive contribution to society.

13. *Development and maintenance of constructive relationships with others at work* (work well with others).
14. *Education* as an important element in the makeup of a well-rounded adult; that it is an integral part of preparation for a socially constructive career that enables the individual to meet his financial needs.
15. *Recognition and acceptance of limited resources and rewards* in lieu of unlimited wants.
16. *Long-range planning and goals are preferred to immediate gratification*; willingness to sacrifice short-term gratification for pursuit of long-term goals.
17. *Personal ownership of property* viewed as basic to human motivation: The individual has the right to accumulate property, to accumulate wealth as a fruit of his work, as a measure of his occupational success.
18. *Freedom of speech and tactfulness* in expressing one's ideas.
19. *Freedom to make decisions about personal goals and daily activities*, including decisions about social, business, civic, and political affiliations to the extent that they do not infringe on the common freedoms of others.
20. *Appreciation of and commitment to a democratic form of government* as demonstrated by (a) a willingness to provide a fair share of financial support (taxes) for the government, (b) development of an understanding of the underlying principles of a democracy, and (c) active participation in the democratic process in a variety of ways, such as educating oneself about issues and candidates in elections, serving in various capacities, and voting.
21. *Privacy in the daily affairs of the individual.*
22. *Appreciation of and commitment to a safe, clean living environment*, beginning in the home and extending to the community, nation, and world.
23. *Personal hygiene and personal grooming* as measures of one's self-respect.
24. *Appreciation and promotion of the arts, traditions, and history as key elements in the promotion of cultural continuity.*
25. *Good mental health and physical health* are treasured.
26. *Recreational activity* is viewed as physically, socially, and emotionally healthy and desirable.

AN EXPANDED ROLE FOR OUR SCHOOLS

Today, however, a more direct role of the school in children's development of values, morals, and character is not enough. Raising children in today's world is much more challenging than it was in the Fifties. Many parents, whether in intact families, single-parent families, divorced families, or remarried families with stepchildren and half siblings, are crying out for help. The role of public schools needs to be expanded and revamped in response to the realities of today and include, among other things, much more help for parents. Specifically, they should provide tax-supported:

1. Services for helping children cope with divorce, stepparents, and other adjustments associated with the modern extended family
2. Guidance and assistance to children in coping with other common problems such as drug abuse, pregnancy, prevention of pregnancy, aggression and violence
3. Programs designed to help high school students understand:
    a. Nature of marriage and personal commitment
    b. Techniques for establishing and maintaining a healthy relationship with a marriage partner through various techniques such as win-win conflict resolution
    c. Virtues of sexual abstinence
    d. Birth control in marriage
    e. Rights of newborn, necessary commitment
    f. Parent training
    g. Setting up and maintaining a family budget
4. Extended-day school programs that provide:
    a. Before-school child care for parents who leave early for work
    b. After-school child care for parents who arrive home from work after regular school hours
    c. Various needs of parents and other adults described below
5. Family counseling services to deal with various matters such as:
    a. Parent-child conflict resolution
    b. Sibling rivalry
    c. Stepchildren, stepparents, stepsiblings, half siblings
    d. Maintaining individual identity within family
    e. Organizational skills for the family and child
6. Expansion of continuing education programs to meet adult needs in:

The Challenge of the New Millennium

  a. Basic skills such as literacy, organizing and maintaining a family budget
  b. General Equivalency Diploma (GED)
  c. New skills such as computer literacy, language
  d. Parenting
  e. Development and clarification of parents' values/morals/ethics
  f. Understanding how to help children develop desirable values and morals
  g. Maintaining a home environment that enhances a child's success at school
7. Referral services for parents and other adults:
  a. Marriage counseling
  b. Coping with divorce, single parenthood, remarriage and stepchildren
  c. Substance abuse, including alcoholism
  d. Unemployment, retraining for job market

What about the cost of these changes. Aren't these services and programs going to cost a great deal? Can we afford them? A better question is: Can we *not* afford them? Consideration of the costs of crime makes the costs of these proposals pale by comparison. And this doesn't include intangibles, such as the deteriorating quality of life and shrinking freedoms—all directly related to our growing fear of crime. I believe that we are now reaping the harvest of societal changes that began in the late Sixties and have continued since: Children who have received inadequate supervision and guidance at home. Disagree? Comparison of the educational and home/family backgrounds of prison inmates with those of the general population is revealing. Inmates' home/family childhood backgrounds include higher incidences of divorced parents, single parents, parents who are poorly educated, alcohol and drug abuse, child neglect and abuse, higher unemployment, and parents with low self-esteem.

Parents need help. The longer implementation of fundamental changes is delayed, the more costly it will be.

Chapter VI

Toward More Responsible Government & A Socially-Compatible, Responsible Citizenry

Some well-meaning policies and assistance programs that are supposed to eliminate or reduce the severity of social and economic problems have actually made matters worse.

Survival of any animal species depends on the ability of each new generation to assume the responsibility of providing for its basic needs. In most advanced species, the young must *learn* some elements essential to survival. A fundamental task of each adult generation, then, is to prepare its young to survive. Among those animals that depend on cooperative efforts to meet their needs, such as the wild dogs of Africa and killer whales, this task takes on added importance: The young must not only learn the general parameters of group-living, they must also learn how to work with others as they strive to meet common needs.

We are not unlike other advanced species in regard to this task. We, too, must teach our young to survive. In a large democratic society in which freedoms and rights of the individual are cherished, this task takes on even greater importance. How so? Like a coin, democracy is two-sided. On the one side is freedom; on the other is personal responsibility. Given the freedom to determine his own destiny within certain social and legal parameters, the individual is expected to accept the responsibility of making his own decisions and living with the consequences. In a democracy, then, freedoms and rights of the individual must be roughly balanced with individual initiative and responsibility.

Public policy should facilitate this process of preparing individuals to be socially-compatible beings who are able to assume responsibility for their own lives. The annual commitment of hundreds of billions of dollars to tuition-free public schools, free lunch programs so poor children have proper nutrition, Head Start, the student loan program for college students, and aid to poor families with dependent children (Aid to Families With Dependent Children—AFDC) are just a few of our efforts to ensure that children have a reasonably good chance of growing up and becoming able to provide for themselves. These efforts are, in a sense, crime prevention measures.

Public policy should also deal effectively with those who drop through the proverbial "cracks" of society and commit unacceptable acts. Efforts to deal with these individuals include spending of billions annually on courts and legal fees, law enforcement agencies that apprehend wrongdoers, rehab programs, and detention facilities.

The question is: How well are these tasks being met? And, is America getting its money's worth? The picture doesn't look good. Today about half of all American families are receiving some type of government assistance[9], the rate of bankruptcies is sky high (880,400 petitions filed in 1991[10]) and growing, and the unemployed demand that unemployment benefits be extended and extended. Nearly one-third of all childbirths are illegitimate, school dropouts continue at an alarming level (nearly 50% in some groups), up to 50% of registered vehicles in some states are not covered with insurance, and our prisons are "maxed out" with those who attempt short cuts to get what they want. Trends are not encouraging. For example, according to a survey released in 1994 by the Bureau of Justice Statistics, in 1980, 139 out of every 100,000 Americans were imprisoned; in 1994 there were 373 out of every 100,000. Apparently, a growing lack of individual responsibility has accompanied the surge of *the beast within*.

This growing tendency toward irresponsibility is also reflected in the federal government. Elected officials often choose to protect spending on their constituents rather than attend to problems in a fiscally responsible manner. Three of the more glaring examples can be found in the soaring national debt, the national park system, and immigration. Officials continue to add billions annually on entitlements and pork barrel projects—while the National Park Service and Border Patrol continue to be grossly underfunded and understaffed. Housing for national park employees is often in a sad state, and illegal aliens enter by the hundreds of thousands each year, often adding to crime problems, further overcrowding schools, and siphoning off much-needed funds for social and health care needs of citizens. How

---

[9] David Hage, D. Fischer, and R. Black. "America's Other Welfare State," *U.S. News & World Report*, April 10, 1995, pp.34-37.

[10] _____, *The American Almanac 1992-1993*, Austin, TX: The Reference Press, Table No. 848, 1992.

does this happen? Amendments to important bills are one way. How so? Whenever there is a legitimate need to appropriate funds for one group, some members of Congress see it as an opportunity to secure funds for their constituents. For example, when Congress appropriated eight billion dollars in assistance for victims of the 1994 earthquake in Los Angeles, amendments to the bill appropriated funds for completely unrelated projects. The eight billion dollars quickly ballooned to eleven billion dollars. Congressmen continue to grab whatever they can for their constituents—seemingly oblivious to the cumulative impact of their individual demands. Concern for the fiscal soundness of the country takes a poor second—if at all. Fairness also takes a back seat. Congressmen in powerful positions sometimes use their power to channel projects to their constituents that go far beyond what many consider to be a fair share. Did the election of a more conservative Congress in November 1994 make a difference? Yes. Will it be enough? The strong push in Congress to balance the federal budget by 2002 and to enact fundamental reforms in welfare is a good start.

Can this growing irresponsibility be attributed to the resurgence of *the beast within*? Of course not. Members of various species have always had to provide for themselves—or perish. What we have today is an artificial situation: Public policies have imposed conditions and circumstances on us that actually make it worthwhile for members, who so choose, to sit back and expect others to provide for them, and for others to victimize innocents with little fear of punishment. Following is an examination of past policies, their effects, and recommended changes where appropriate.

A Fundamental Change

Up until the 1930s, private charities set up and operated by churches, organizations, and individuals provided most of the assistance to those in need. This was in part, no doubt, a result of our religious heritage. But it also was a product of life on the frontier and life in rural communities where people often "pitched in" to help their neighbors, whether it was a barn-raising or taking care of a neighbor's livestock or crops during illness. This was the age of *real* charity—not just the tax write-off.

Today most of the funds to care for those in need and to prepare the next generation to take care of itself come from other sources: primarily income taxes and property taxes on individuals and businesses, and social insurance taxes. When did this change begin?

States began setting up tax-supported public schools in the 1830s. Tariffs on imported goods and bonds provided some funds. But the availability of funds didn't really open up until 1913 when the 16th Amendment provided a solid legal footing for an income tax. (The personal income tax was first instituted during the Civil War.) It was eventually to become a source of funds limited only by Congressmen's fears of angry constituents.

What prompted this change from private charities to public financing of assistance programs? The Great Depression of the 1930s. Millions were out of work, millions were losing their homes and farms because they could not make mortgage payments, and millions were hungry. Many soon came to believe that private business and private charity simply could not adequately deal with this new challenge. "The government has to do something!" became a common cry.

Initially a luxury tax, the federal income tax became a *progressive* income tax during World War I. In doing so, it became the financial basis for a fundamental change in regard to the role of government: that government should play an *active* role in determining the quality of life of the individual. It also marked the acceptance of the idea that government has the right, even the duty, to transfer wealth from the *haves* to the *have nots*, that redistribution of wealth through tax policy is a legitimate way of providing assistance to those who have less.

The presidential election of 1932 focused on the hardships of people and how to deal with them. The Democratic ticket proposed a much more active role for the federal government. Rightly or wrongly, the domestic policies of the Hoover Administration were blamed by the Democratic ticket as the cause of the economic crisis—and most voters bought it. The Democratic ticket won handily. Franklin D. Roosevelt was sworn in as the next president and the New Deal quickly began taking shape during his "first 100 days."

Sweeping changes began to go into effect. Programs such as the Civilian Conservation Corps (CCC) were implemented to put people back to work, banking reforms and the Federal Deposit Insurance Corporation (FDIC) put banks on a more sound footing and provided protection for depositors, and other programs such as the Rural Electrification Administration (REA) were implemented to improve the general living conditions of people. The Farm Credit Administration provided mortgage relief for farmers, and the Federal Housing Administration (FHA) insured mortgages for new construction and home repairs. The Agricultural Adjustment Administration, then the

Agricultural Adjustment Act helped farmers by providing funds for soil conservation, reduction of production, raising prices on certain crops to "parity" (subsidies), and crop loans. The Social Security Act improved workers' welfare by establishing an assistance program for the aged, vocational rehabilitation, and uniform unemployment compensation. It also provided aid for the blind, homeless and crippled children and assistance for dependent mothers and children. A food stamp program implemented in 1939 provided agricultural commodities to persons on relief. It should be noted that, where practical, the work ethic embedded in the American psyche led policy makers to require participants in programs to work for assistance rather than just be given handouts. This was incorporated, for example, in the CCC and in the WPA.

The measures taken in the Social Security Act of 1935 constituted the beginning of major government intervention in the welfare of the individual. President Lyndon B. Johnson, a protégé of FDR, sought in the 1960s to continue and expand in his "Great Society" many of the ideas initiated by FDR. His "Job Corps" bore a close resemblance to parts of the New Deal. Significantly, the programs of the Great Society continued to assume responsibility for the welfare of the individual.

What was the basis of these public assistance policies? It was apparently two-fold. As in other developed countries, Americans have long been noted for their compassion and willingness to help those in need. There was, then, a genuine concern for the well-being of the unemployed and the homeless in the midst of the depression. Early on, however, many believed that private charities and private business would adequately provide for the needy. But as more and more lost their jobs and breadlines became commonplace, many began to argue that private charities and business could not adequately provide for the millions in need. Although it arrived late in the depression, John Steinbeck's *The Grapes of Wrath* strengthened the resolve of many to help the less fortunate. Indeed, the unemployment rate that shot up in the early 1930s remained at 17% even in 1939 when Steinbeck's highly acclaimed novel appeared. The programs of the New Deal undoubtedly provided assistance to millions who, like those in Steinbeck's novel, were in *serious* need.

But another basis for these policies and programs soon became apparent—and it is more apparent today. As in many other species, a symbiotic relationship normally exists in a human society between the ruler and the ruled. The leader enjoys certain powers and privileges, and provides benefits for his subjects. His subjects enjoy those benefits, pay taxes, and are loyal to him. And as long as each enjoys the expected benefits, they have a vested interest in maintaining the status quo. Such a relationship is especially obvious in America today between the people and their elected leaders. How did this happen? The lucrative salaries, retirement benefits, and perks that they have bestowed on themselves make being a member of Congress or president more attractive than ever. Predictably, once in office, they want to stay in office.

How have incumbents enhanced their chances of re-election? They have always based their appeal to their constituents on what they've been doing *for* them—and that the job is not finished. (They usually try to hide what they do for themselves.) Promises that have traditionally had popular appeal include: More jobs! Affordable housing! Lower taxes! (If necessary, tax the "rich" or raise them on the other guy.) Less crime! Extended unemployment benefits! Support for poor families with dependent children! Free lunch programs! People have, as a result, come to expect more and more *from* their government, and assistance programs that began in the 1930s have been expanding ever since. Today more and more of us are *entitled* to them! Why? Aside from any legitimate need, politicians quickly discovered that, like pork barrel projects, providing "benefits" for their constituents was one of the best ways of securing re election. How so? As citizens accept public assistance, they become dependent on it. They need their representatives to continue the assistance, and since their representatives need their votes for re-election, assistance continues. This symbiotic relationship, despite its apparent immediate benefits to those directly involved, is ultimately destructive. Recipients become dependents of government, and the fiscal soundness of America is undermined as elected officials continue to add unnecessarily to the national debt. Is the purpose of our government to make citizens dependents? Of course not—at least historically! One of the goals of a democracy based on free enterprise is to allow the individual to be responsible for himself.

THE DOWNSIDE OF PUBLIC ASSISTANCE PROGRAMS

Since the New Deal of the 1930s, we have been expanding the government's role in being responsible *for* the individual as individual responsibilities have been redefined as "rights," "guarantees," and "entitlements." The Clinton administration's assertion in 1993 that comprehensive health care was a "right" that all Americans are "entitled" to was an attempt to continue this trend. But with this expanding role as guardian and provider for the individual, a growing number of Americans have embraced the status of being a dependent: Today about half of all American families are receiving some type of public assistance. Growing numbers of young, single women with children are on assistance, and more and more individuals are on Supplemental Security Income (SSI).

But aren't assistance programs supposed to help recipients become self-supporting, independent citizens? Yes, this should be the goal, but some programs, as they have been structured and implemented, have done the opposite. That is, they have made matters worse. They have had a detrimental impact on the lives of those they are supposed to help and, in such cases, have been ultimately destructive to society as a whole. How so? Aid to Families With Dependent Children (AFDC) is one example. AFDC has provided long-term assistance to poor, single mothers for *each* child that they have had—without limit. Seldom have there been any requirements regarding continued enrollment in high school, job training, reciprocal work, or parent training. For many young women with no marketable job skills because they dropped out of school, having children has been an irresistible means of income. Today, as a result, we see growing numbers of families on AFDC, with unmarried and poorly educated single mothers having children, generation after generation. Statistics verify this trend: Total illegitimate births as a percentage of all births in the United States have risen from 5% in 1960 to about 30% in 1992—and they continue to increase. Children relying on AFDC have grown from just over two million in 1960 to about 10 million today! Put in perspective, while the total population of the United States hasn't even doubled since 1960, children on AFDC have increased five-fold. Why? Assistance policies have actually undermined the intent of the program. Poor, single women have been, in effect, encouraged to drop out of school and give birth to children that they do not want and can not provide for. The worst part is that we now have countless children from poor, single-parent families, often neglected and abused, who become easy victims or new recruits of a destructive street culture of drugs and violence. And many of them grow up resentful and angry, ready to attack others to get what they want. We hear about their crimes every day from the media. This is not to imply that all assistance from AFDC and other programs is wasted. But fundamental reforms are clearly needed.

The Challenge of the New Millennium

There are more drawbacks to assistance programs. For example, once a program and its bureaucracy are established, they tend to develop a life of their own and continue beyond the period when there was a legitimate need for the assistance. For example, price supports that were started in the 1930s to assist mostly small farmers continue to guarantee prices for agricultural products and force consumers to spend billions annually in inflated prices. The wool and dairy subsidies continue. And the peanut quota system allows a farmer to produce his quota or sit back and rent it to someone else. Even worse, much of the financial support goes not into the pockets of small farmers, but into the pockets of a relatively few large producers who really don't need it.

Assistance programs, once established, also grow in scope and cost. Bilingual education is one example. Its original goal was to enable non-English-speaking immigrant children who enrolled in public schools to become fluent in English as soon as possible so they could be moved into the English-speaking mainstream curriculum. It provided bilingual teachers and classes for such students. Today bilingual education is much more. It addresses broader cultural concerns and even includes teaching non-immigrant children a foreign language. (This, of course, provides more jobs for those in bilingual education.) Not surprisingly, it has grown from a budget of $7.5 million in 1968 to nearly $10 billion today. Another example is Social Security. The Social Security Act of 1935 provided assistance for the aged and the unemployed, relief for the destitute blind and dependent children, and funds for services in "public health work, vocational rehabilitation, and maternity and infant care."[11] Enacted during a deep economic crisis, it apparently was envisioned as a safety net and included a series of programs that were to provide the minimum needed by individuals who qualified. Then there was the Social Security Act of 1939, the Social Security Act of 1950, the Social Security Act of 1952, and so on. Significantly, each act increased benefits and/or changed the qualifications so additional people could qualify. Changes invariably entitled more people to receive assistance. Today, for example, even the retired wealthy receive monthly Social Security checks and Medicare assistance that often eventually amount to far more than they contributed, including

---

[11] Richard B. Morris, ed. *Encyclopedia of American History*, rev & enlarged ed., New York: Harper & Row (1961), pp.352-353.

accrued interest. Apparently, these programs are more than just safety nets that provide for those in real need.

Nationwide assistance programs that are centrally controlled also require establishment of large bureaucracies—which often leads to mismanagement or poor management. "Red tape" typically slows processing, overall efficiency, and follow-up and closure to individual cases. The college student loan program is a good example. Despite the dismal record of repayment and the growing amount of unpaid loans with billions added annually, student loans continue to be provided essentially on an on-demand basis. Who's to worry about repayment? Not the program administrators. They continue to receive their salaries. Nor the banks who set up the loans. They receive their funds when the loan is approved. Guess who covers the bad loans!

And this leads to another problem common to many large programs—especially those created by Congress: Programs often do not include sufficient numbers of "worker bees" in the field. That is, Congress often creates new programs, but fails to fund sufficient field workers to make it work. This is apparent, for example, in assistance for the disabled from Supplemental Security Income (SSI). Inadequate staffing and supervision sometimes results in drug addicts and alcoholics spending assistance on more drugs or booze. This is also the case in many other efforts of Congress. For example, inadequate funding of the Immigration and Naturalization Service and staffing of our Border Patrol has resulted in about three million illegal aliens residing in the United States, with an influx of about 300,000 more each year![12] This influx costs far more in health care, education, and social services than adequate funding of the Immigration and Naturalization Service would require. Likewise, funding for the national park system has provided neither adequate personnel nor decent housing for National Park Service employees. Predictably, legislation expanding the national park system in 1994 did not include funds for additional personnel or housing for personnel.

Another shortcoming of public assistance programs is related to cost of operations. Salaries of administrators and top level staff often soak up most of the funds that are supposed to help the targeted group. The Teacher Corps was a good example. Most of the appropriated funds were spent on salaries for administrators and supportive

---

[12] James Popkin and Dorian Friedman, "Return to Sender—Please," *U.S. News & World Report* 114 (June 21, 1993), p.32.

staff at the national level and in local projects. Direct assistance to undergraduate students in training to be teachers and teachers being "retrained" at the graduate level accounted for a fraction of the total budget.

Still another problem with public assistance programs is related to management. In some programs, once an individual is admitted to an assistance program, benefits go on and on without limit. Assistance becomes a way of life since the individual is "entitled" to it. Does this encourage the individual to provide for himself? Of course not. As a matter of fact, programs for the able-bodied that do not have limits have the opposite effect! They encourage participants to be irresponsible, to be *dependent* on society.

There is yet another facet to this downside of public assistance programs. Where do the funds for these programs come from? There are two primary sources: taxes and public debt. We either raise taxes on today's taxpayers, or we raise them on tomorrow's taxpayers by piling up more national debt. Of course we're doing both. But we can't continue to pile up national debt. Crunch time is approaching. Without *real* elimination of annual federal deficits, the national debt will soon reach a point where servicing it (paying the interest) will consume most revenues. As a matter of fact, servicing the debt is already the largest single expenditure in our budget! Entitlement programs alone, if allowed to continue expanding, will add increasingly large amounts to the national debt. And we can't blame defense spending anymore—it has already been significantly reduced. What we must do is get a handle on entitlement programs—across the board, and greatly reduce the pork barrel projects. Otherwise, America will continue to grow as a nation of dependents rather than as a nation of responsible individuals—and bankrupt itself.

WHERE WE GO FROM HERE

Most Americans believe that there are legitimate needs for assistance programs, especially during periods of widespread economic hardship. The Civilian Conservation Corps and Works Progress Administration of the 1930s, for example, provided much needed jobs for millions, thereby enabling participants to maintain their dignity as well as a source of income. Continuance of these types of programs during economic hard times is clearly in the best interest of the nation as well as those individuals who participate. But if truly lasting help is to be provided for those in need, assistance programs should enable recipients to *become* able to provide for themselves.

Programs, then, should require recipients to enroll in and complete on a timely basis tax-supported education and job training programs in *meaningful* careers as conditions for financial support for housing, food, health care, and other daily needs such as child care when working or receiving training. Such an arrangement will provide the best chance for the recipient of assistance to become self-supporting. This approach is in keeping with the philosophy that guided many programs of the 1930s, such as the National Youth Administration. If we do otherwise, that is, provide unlimited assistance without equipping them to provide a better life for themselves, we simply entrap them in their current state. In such case, our compassion and efforts are destructive rather than helpful.

Obviously, two types of assistance programs are needed: (1) those that provide long-term assistance to individuals who are unable to become self-supporting, such as the aged and individuals with permanent physical or mental limitations, and (2) those that provide *temporary* assistance to individuals who are able to learn to take care of themselves. The following suggested changes should be more acceptable since they include sacrifices by participants in several programs. If enacted, the changes would require individuals to be more responsible for themselves, would reduce the frequency of victimization of innocents, and likely contribute to the fiscal soundness of the country.

We also need to face the reality of how family life has changed and deal with it as effectively as possible. This means accepting divorced and single-parent families as part of reality and providing support systems for those types of families. This does not imply that we ignore the needs of today's traditional families. On the contrary, we need to implement policies and support systems that promote the traditional family as the most desirable home environment for raising children. These efforts should include tax-supported services that are designed to save traditional marriages from "going on the rocks," where possible, and thereby reduce the remarriages and stepchildren, half brothers and half sisters, and shuffling of children from parent to parent in today's version of the extended family. They should also include school programs that are designed to help teens develop realistic expectations of marriage and parenthood.

We must also deal with an even more fundamental change in society that has occurred since the Fifties. Today we constantly hear about freedoms and rights of the individual. Indeed, Americans enjoy and cherish freedoms and rights as individuals in few other societies

The Challenge of the New Millennium

do. But somewhere along the way, individual responsibility has clearly taken a back seat. America has become to a considerable extent a nation of buck-passers where many do not want to be accountable. Shouts of, "It's my right!" and threats to sue seem to have left less and less room for individual responsibility. This skewed emphasis on freedoms and rights has been reinforced by the ever-expanding list of entitlements declared by the federal government. This *must* change. The natural balance between freedoms and rights, on the one hand, and individual responsibility, on the other, needs to be re-established. To accomplish this, I propose the establishment of the American Civil Responsibilities Association (ACRA) to spearhead this effort. Specific objectives of this organization could include:

1. Identification of desirable individual responsibilities.
2. Identification of desirable civic responsibilities.
3. Creation and implementation of school programs designed to help children develop a sense of individual and civic responsibility.
4. Inclusion of support groups and learning experiences designed to help parents promote the development of a sense of individual responsibility in their children.
5. Organization and recruitment of individuals to assume civic responsibilities, such as helping to conduct elections, community cleanup efforts, school volunteers, and security patrols.
6. Publication of public service announcements, magazine articles, and other materials that promote individual and civic responsibility among our citizens.
7. Linkage and coordination of efforts of various existing organizations to promote civic and community service.

Political Reforms

But first, for the reason alluded to earlier, political reforms must be a high priority. During the posturing about the Clinton administration's reforms in 1993, some conservative House members insisted on "entitlement caps." The final agreement was: If entitlement expenditures exceed certain targets, government must raise taxes or cut spending or do nothing. What happened was more public debt. This was one of the much talked about "hard choices?" What it was, was just another example of the failure of elected officials to make any serious effort to face up to the financial difficulty confronting America. What we have, as a result, are financial and social crises looming on the horizon that politicians helped create—and who seem unable or unwilling to deal with in a responsible manner. Did the budget agreement of 1993 mark the beginning of significant reductions in our annual deficits? It did result in a reduction of our annual deficits. But projections of the Clinton administration in 1995 indicated that these reductions were only temporary. According to those projections, the federal deficit would exceed $200 billion in 1996 and continue to grow thereafter, exceeding $300 billion in 2001. And these were *deficits*—not surpluses. Such fiscal irresponsibility is outrageous. What is needed are balanced budgets—even surpluses. Otherwise, America is headed for a financial meltdown—high inflation, high interest rates, and a collapse of the dollar. (Actually, the value of the dollar is already collapsing. Prices of automobiles, for example, have more than quadrupled since 1970.) Fortunately, a more conservative Congress began a more fiscally-responsible path in 1995. The problem is, with one eye on re-election, few elected officials, despite our deficits, seem eager to cut a program that affects a significant number of their constituents.

The failure of Congress to pass the balanced budget amendment in 1995, the sixth time since 1982, deepened the pessimism of many. Opponents, led by President Clinton, managed to defeat the amendment despite polls indicating over 70% of the people supported the amendment. (Who's to worry about *of the people, by the people, and for the people*?) Protection of the Social Security Trust Fund was one of the excuses used to defeat the amendment in the Senate—despite the bipartisan report that Social Security would eventually face bankruptcy without fundamental change and the fact that surpluses in the Social Security Fund were already being used to mask the deficit's true size. (The Council for Government Reform estimates the federal government is borrowing over $50 billion each year from the fund to cover other spending—which totaled nearly half a trillion dollars by 1995.) Another excuse was concern about "tampering" with the Constitution—despite the fact that we already have twenty-seven amendments. Obviously, these were *excuses*—not reasons. The truth is, opponents fought hard against it because they saw it as a threat to their ability to fund entitlements, or saw it as part of a strategy to embarrass the Republican leadership and, at the same time, position themselves for the 1996 elections. This is supported by the fact that most of those who voted against the amendment were the same ones who continually cried about deficit spending during the Reagan and Bush administrations—yet failed to make any major re-

The Challenge of the New Millennium

forms in entitlements to reduce the growth of spending during those 12 years. Or during the first two years of the Clinton administration.

The partisan bickering will continue. Why? It's the nature of politics in a democracy, especially in today's America. The desire for *power* and its benefits is simply irresistible. Opposing parties often "trash" each other as they seek political advantage. They present their views as favorably as possible as they attempt to discredit those of their opponents through a variety of tactics: appeals to patriotism, statistics, scare tactics, exaggerations, lies, and other forms of propaganda. The drive for political advantage may even supersede leadership. For example, the absence of major reductions in the growth of spending in the budget that President Clinton submitted to Congress in early 1995 was clearly a ploy of the president to position himself for the 1996 elections. In doing so, he forced the Republican-controlled Congress to propose the reductions and take the blame of those whose interests were impacted. Predictably, he was among the first to attack the reductions. He asserted, for example, that the Republican-proposed reduction in the growth of spending on Medicare (from 11% annually to 6 or 7%) was a "cut" that would "destroy" Medicare—despite the fact that he and the first lady had proposed a similar reduction in 1993 and 1994 and pointed out that it was "not a cut" but "a reduction in the growth of spending." Likewise, despite our annual deficits, the Republicans sought votes by pushing a tax cut in their "Contract for America." But the 1994 elections were a wakeup call for President Clinton. Not to be outdone in 1996, he reversed himself (again) after the 1994 elections and began advocating a tax cut in his "Bill of Rights for the Middle Class." (Clinton promised no new taxes for the middle class in his 1992 campaign, led the fight for the large tax increase in 1993, then, in 1995, advocated a tax cut for the middle class.) Apparently the prevailing principle is: Do whatever is politically expedient—even if it means a budget impasse and a government shut down. Voters need to remember that political one-upmanship serves not the people, but those who wish to gain an advantage in the ongoing struggle for *power*.

Even more disturbing, however, is the erosion of the trust and confidence of the people in their elected leaders and in the democratic process. Party loyalty and, as illustrated above, political advantage often take priority over sound fiscal policy and integrity. Flip-flops by politicians who promise one thing in their campaigns when seeking votes, then reverse themselves after entering office are especially corrosive. The battle over the balanced budget amendment in 1995, for example, resulted in flip-flops by several senators, including Feinstein of California, Hollings of South Carolina, and Bingaman of New Mexico. Likewise, some candidates for Congress in 1994 supported term limits for Congress in their campaigns, then changed their minds after being elected. No wonder public confidence in some elected leaders is so low. As credibility and integrity go south, so do public confidence and trust. But the real danger lies not in the loss of confidence in individuals, but in their cumulative effect—the loss of confidence in a democratic form of government.

Fairness, however, requires a broader view of the causes of excessive federal spending. The federal deficits of the 1980s and the 1990s aren't entirely the fault of elected officials. We need to look in the mirror. Yes, we, the people, are a fundamental factor in the growing mountain of national debt. Our annual deficits are essentially the result of the growing expectations of those who are receiving benefits—and the rest of us who sit by and watch spending grow. As noted earlier, in 1994 about half of all households received benefits. And most of these weren't poor. $177 billion was spent on entitlements for the poor; $612 billion was received by the rest of us—for Social Security, Medicare, mortgage interest deductions, veterans' benefits, agricultural subsidies, unemployment compensation, and so on.[13] And in most cases, the higher the income bracket, the greater the tax break or payment. Recipients of Social Security checks *expect* payments to continue—in full, even when payments eventually exceed total contributions to the fund and interest. Ditto recipients of Medicare, farm subsidies, tax breaks for business, Medicaid, AFDC, and so on. Polls indicate that reduction of the deficit is more important than tax cuts, and that most Americans believe that the growth of spending on assistance must be reduced. But the problem is, most of us want to cut *other* programs, not ours. If federal deficits, are to be eliminated, we must realize that everything—including Social Security, must be on the table. Fairness demands that reductions in the growth of spending in all areas should be affected. There are no attractive alternatives.

There's also a matter of morality. Is it right for us to enjoy costly benefits today that future generations will have to pay for? Of course not. Unchecked deficit spending, especially for things that many

---

[13] David Hage, D. Fischer, and R. Black. "America's Other Welfare State," *U.S. News & World Report* (April 10, 1995), pp.34-37.

could do without, is wrong. As individuals, we wouldn't think of buying something today that our children and grandchildren would have to pay for. But this is what we are doing as a society. Future generations are going to have to pay our bills—in higher taxes, higher inflation, and higher interest rates. They will have to do without tomorrow because of what was selfishly demanded today. But we take as much as possible because "everybody else is" and because national debt seems rather impersonal. We need to wake up. The national debt is personal. It affects everyone. And it will affect our children and their children. It is nothing more than passing today's bills on to them. But President Clinton, despite his 1992 campaign pledge to balance the budget in five years, initially opposed the Republican plan to balance the budget in seven years, claiming that such a timetable would require "inhumane cuts" in social and health care programs. He advocated, instead, to balance the federal budget in ten years. In other words, dumping ten more years of bills onto our children and grandchildren was acceptable. What kind of compassion is this? The reality is, compassion and balancing the federal budget were not his primary concerns in late 1995. His primary concern was, rather, his appearance as protector of programs of those who might support his re-election.

But there's another factor that is seldom mentioned by today's Democrats or Republicans: the aging of America. As America moves into the 21st century, its population will continue to age. That is, the elderly will comprise a larger and larger percentage of our population—and taxpaying workers will make up a smaller and smaller portion. This will accelerate as the wave of babyboomers reaches retirement during the first three decades of the 21st century. Fewer and fewer working taxpayers will have to support more and more retirees. Sooner or later, Social Security will have to be addressed. But for fear of losing the votes of today's retirees, neither Republicans nor Democrats have proposed reductions in the growth of Social Security expenditures. They have avoided Social Security like the plague. The problem is, this bear isn't going to walk away into the forest. It's going to grow bigger and bigger. And the longer serious adjustments are delayed, the higher the tax rate on tomorrow's taxpayers. Without serious adjustments soon, tomorrow's taxpayers will be paying at least 82% or more of their income in taxes. Their economic freedom will be lost as they become slaves to those who are retired. They will rightly conclude that they were robbed and refuse to pay such taxes. Today's retirees should wake up and accept a slower rate of growth in Social Security outlays. Otherwise, retirees of the early 21st century will face *major* reductions—or rebellion.

Fortunately, in 1995 more fiscally-responsible leadership emerged in the Congress. But fundamental change in government is never easy. And the move toward fiscally-responsible government and policies to promote individual responsibility has proved to be difficult. Efforts to slow the expansion of spending in entitlements have been resisted at nearly every turn by those who want to protect the expansion of entitlements—and enhance their chances of re-election.

America deserves leadership in the president and in Congress that focuses on governing in a *responsible* manner, not on the struggle to acquire or retain power. This means focusing on serving the long-range interests of the people—*and* paying the bills. Leaders should understand the problems confronting society and have the courage to deal with these problems in a straightforward manner—even when it means telling the people what they don't want to hear. Candidates should clearly specify their principles and intentions in campaigns. Once in office, they should keep campaign promises and maintain a steady course in leadership. Officials should also have vision and a sense of mission as we look to the future, and give us hope and inspire us to achieve. They should be willing to take bold steps, yet exemplify humility in their leadership. Above all, leaders should display a high level of integrity and ask no more of others than they have given of themselves. Unfortunately, America often gets less, and there is no way of totally eliminating the flip-flops, the demagoguery, the arrogance, and the lack of integrity in politics today.

Is it possible to improve the quality of candidates and leadership in America? Possibly, but freedom of speech and the right of anyone to run for office in a democracy leaves the door open to all types of individuals. And those of questionable character aren't always screened in lower offices or primaries. However, several reforms might improve the odds of securing more responsible leadership. But before offering specific reforms, some basic facts about how *power* and the pursuit of *power* affect politicians and the political process need to be recognized. They are:

— *The pursuit of power is a primary force that drives politics.* The adulation and privileges bestowed on leaders reveal the mesmerizing effect of power and power figures. Add the generous perks, allowances, and retirement benefits, and pursuit of power posi-

tions becomes irresistible. Candidates and officeholders constantly maneuver for advantage in public opinion as they pursue power.
— *The pursuit of power supersedes issues.* Issues come and go, but the pursuit of power continues. Indeed, issues of the day are mere vehicles that politicians use to catapult themselves into power positions. Although philosophical differences affect *how* issues are addressed, it is power that is the prize.
— *Power is intoxicating.* It is exciting, feels good. Once experienced, it is self-perpetuating, difficult to let go of. (This is the basis for the campaign chant, "Four more years!" and why incumbents in high office are rarely satisfied with one term.)
— *Power inflates one's ego.* The greater an official's power, privileges, and adulation, the more likely he will see himself not as the servant, but as the master, and view his intellect and ideas as superior, those of others inferior. When an official feels great power, he may see himself rise above constraints placed on ordinary people.
— *Power is corrupting.* Those who acquire power and privilege tend to see staff and supporters ("worker bees") as resources or objects to be used, even abused; they are tempted to take advantage of admirers since they believe they have risen above retribution. They may accept offers for personal gain from supporters in exchange for favors. The greater the power, the greater the temptations and chances of corruption; the longer an individual holds power, the more likely he will be corrupted.
— *The pursuit of power (and party unity) may supersede sound management of a nation's business.* Efforts of incumbents to secure and maintain support of constituents account for most deficit spending, burgeoning assistance programs, and pork barrel projects. Individual party members are sometimes forced to set aside personal misgivings about an issue or bill in order to maintain party unity (power). Party leaders may also instruct members to oppose a bill in order to embarrass leadership of an opposing party.
— *Power rewards loyalty.* Those who are loyal, who contribute more to a candidate or leader are rewarded first—and most. Those who do not contribute or are disloyal, are ignored, demoted, or punished otherwise.

Given that the pursuit of power is a primary force behind those who seek high positions, it seems prudent to draw some basic assumptions about individuals who seek such positions in a highly competitive political environment. They usually:

— Have inflated egos. They believe that their intellect and ideas are better (superior), that they should lead and others should follow, that they *deserve* a place in history.
— Exude self-confidence and decisiveness.
— Have an exaggerated desire to control others.
— Have an exceptional ability to "read" people—their fears and hopes, and how to manipulate public opinion.
— Are exceptional orators. They can articulate ideas more effectively and can persuade listeners that they can lead, that their ideas are best for society.
— Are able to sense the moods and desires of people, and address issues appropriately.
— See power positions as opportunities for social and financial enrichment, not just in salary, perks, and allowances while in office, but also in retirement benefits, perks, and contacts for other income opportunities after leaving office.

How can a society secure better representation in government and protect itself from tyranny? First, voters need to stay well-informed and maintain a healthy skepticism toward those in power positions. Judgments about politicians, then, should be based on what they have done, not on what they say. Voters need to be able to sift through the chaff and bombast, spot flip-flops, demagoguery, half-truths, and outright lies when they occur, and have longer memories when they go to the polls. They also need to be able to recognize manipulative techniques often used by politicians. Some of the most frequently used are:

— Appeals to patriotism
— Emotional appeals to convince voters that he cares ("the children," "the poor," ...)
— Bandwagon: Scenes of large groups of enthusiastic supporters suggest everybody is joining up! Even celebrities ("beautiful people") may be recruited to appear next to a candidate. (This explains why party conventions usually give the nominee a boost in the polls.)
— Repetition: Repeat something enough—whether it is a candidate's name or a statement that is based on a false premise—and many will eventually accept it.

The Challenge of the New Millennium 153

— Cite favorable examples and statistics, ignore those that are unfavorable
— Maintain high visibility with political ads and photo ops, such as signings of documents, press conferences, and press releases
— Pork barrel: Approve projects, grants, contracts to local businesses that translate into jobs and an improved local economy or services
— Speeches to selected groups that will receive the candidate with great enthusiasm (while cameras are rolling, of course)
— Claim credit for achievements others—many will accept it as fact
— Distort opponent's position—again, many will accept it as fact
— Ignore constructive accomplishments of opponent
— When unfavorable information is publicized, ignore it, attack the messenger instead

Political reforms can also make a difference. What reforms are most obviously needed in America today? First, safeguards need to be put in place. They should include:

— Absolute limit on length of time an individual can serve in a given position of power.
— Division of powers spread among different branches of government—legislative, executive, and judicial.
— Absolute limits on emergency powers of the chief executive and on the length of time those powers can be in force.
— Personal estate of anyone elected to high position placed in a blind trust *before* taking office.
— Prohibition of elected leaders serving as lobbyists after leaving office.
— No golden parachutes upon completion of service in high position—no lucrative retirement, severance plans, etc. Only a modest franking allowance provided for those who have served as president, vice-president, in Congress, and on the Supreme Court.
— Predetermined process for removing from office any official who commits unconstitutional acts.

With these safeguards in mind, what reforms need to be made? Obviously, the writers of the Constitution addressed some of the above concerns. But developments during the last few decades indicate a need for others. Those that seem most obvious include:

— Reduce politicians' fixation on getting re-elected. The constitutional amendment limiting anyone to two terms as president provides precedent. Limitation of anyone to two terms in Congress will reduce the time that groups or individuals with special links to a given Congressman can unduly impact legislation; it will eliminate the tendency of members with long tenure to wield unreasonable power over colleagues; it will also enable Congressmen to focus more on serving the people, rather than themselves, and weigh the impact of their decisions more on the nation as a whole.

— Eliminate retirement plans for elected and appointed federal officials. While in office, then, officials are to continue their contributions to the general Social Security fund and/or any private fund in which they are a participant.
— Set strict limits on campaign spending for federal offices. These limits must be approved by popular vote of the people.
— Finance campaigns for federal offices with public funds (taxes), and prohibit contributions of all kinds from PACS and all other private sources.
— Prohibit the acceptance of gifts and fees of all kinds by elected and/or appointed federal officials. Acceptance of trips or vacations disguised as speaking engagements, "working trips," "fact-finding trips," trips for acceptance of awards, and similar rewards from special interest groups should also be prohibited. Violation should be sufficient ground for immediate removal from office.
— Except for the Secretary of State and the Secretary of Defense, limit publicly-funded travel abroad of each member of Congress and each member of the Cabinet to 18 days annually. Public funds for such travel of each official, including airfare and support staff, shall be limited to $36,000 annually. However, an additional $12,000 may be available for security personnel for each official.
— Prohibit elected or appointed federal and state officials serving as lobbyists after leaving office.
— Amend the Constitution so that pay raises, increases in benefits, and perks of elected and appointed officials at the federal level must be approved by the voters.
— Provide a line-item veto for the president of the United States in budgetary matters that requires a two-thirds majority vote by Congress to be overridden. (The line-item veto passed in 1996 required a simple majority and was restricted to certain areas.)

Obviously, the first of the above recommended changes will require considerable effort. It will require a constitutional amendment.

The Challenge of the New Millennium

But the 22nd Amendment, which limited the maximum terms for the presidency to two, provides precedent. The problem is, getting Congress to restrict itself likewise. As demonstrated by its repeated refusal to pass a balanced budget amendment, it will resist changes that restrict its power. There is, however distasteful, a way of enhancing the attractiveness of term limits to today's members of Congress: Exempt those currently in office from the limitation. But even with this change, passage of a constitutional amendment that limits terms for Congressmen will not be easy. (Of course, there is always the option of doing as one bumper sticker advocated: "Re-elect nobody.") Once this change is made, other reforms, such as a balanced budget amendment, will be much easier to enact.

Entitlement Policies & Other Policies

What reforms need to be made in entitlements and other give-away policies? First, a look at some of the current policies and programs that cause individuals to become dependent on others and behave in socially-destructive ways. It should be noted, however, that the following list is by no means inclusive; it includes only a few of the more widely known current policies and conditions:

— Overburdened police and courts and overcrowded prisons result in violent offenders being put on probation or granted early parole—free to prey on society again and again. (Even "three strikes and you're out" allows the violent offender three *(three!)* victims before being put away permanently.)

— A rather ineffective system for following up and collecting from those who receive federal student loans allows many to avoid following through with financial agreements.

— AFDC encourages poor families and single women, in effect, to have an unlimited number of children that they cannot provide for. The worst part is that some of these children are unwanted and unloved, are not taught basic skills, amenities, or culturally-compatible values, and are neglected or abused—prime ingredients of youngsters who grow up angry to prey on society as adults.

— In most states single, poorly educated and unemployed parents on AFDC are not required to enroll in any program that will enable them to develop or enhance their job skills. Even worse, they often have no access to parenting programs or do not take advantage of such programs.

— Individuals who are disabled because of alcoholism or drug addiction and children who are classified as disabled may each receive monthly payments upwards of $400 from Supplemental Security Income (SSI). Although the payment to the alcoholic or drug addict is supposed to be received by a responsible individual who is to supervise use of the funds, payments often go to another addict or someone else, such as a friendly bartender, who simply gives the check to the alcoholic or addict who, in turn, uses the funds to buy more booze or drugs. SSI has also resulted in a growing number of children who, after being instructed by their parents to act unusual or misbehave in the presence of the examining doctor, are being wrongly classified as disabled simply to qualify for the funds. (Total cash benefit payments from SSI for the disabled grew from $3.1 billion in 1975 to $12.5 billion in 1990.[14])
— School dropouts and high school graduates often have received little or no preparation for marriage and parenthood, whether it is setting up and maintaining a family budget, maintaining a healthy relationship with a marriage partner, or establishing an emotionally healthy atmosphere for children.
— Capable individuals are allowed to drop out of high school—with the 21st century staring them in the face! They then complain about economic and social injustice and demand, despite their lack of marketable job skills, "a good job." (Although graduation rates are improving, a dropout rate approaching 50% continues in one large ethnic group.)
— Individuals who choose to drop out of high school and significantly lower their chances of providing for themselves may qualify for assistance.
— Medicare provides assistance for those who are wealthy.
— Upper income individuals qualify for and receive monthly Social Security retirement benefits—often even beyond what they contributed during their working years. As a matter of fact, payments to the typical retiree consume all accumulated contributions and interest during the first three to five years. Payments received after the first few years, then, are, in reality, welfare.
— The funding of programs to train or retrain the unemployed is very limited (less than 1% of federal outlays) and *declining*!

---

[14] ____, *The American Almanac 1992-1993*, Austin, TX: The Reference Press, Table No. 593, 1992.

The Challenge of the New Millennium

- Many "deadbeat fathers" do not provide court-ordered support for their children.
- The justice system is unable to prevent a divorced parent from kidnapping his/her child from the parent granted custody.
- Serious family conflict and child abuse may continue for years without therapeutic intervention by professionals trained to help families deal with them.
- Most expectant parents are inadequately prepared to be parents in today's challenging world.
- There are few tax-supported counseling programs available to help families cope with divorce, re-marriage and relationships in the modern extended family, and single-parenthood.
- Divorce laws allow parents to get divorced rather easily. For example, those contemplating divorce are not required to participate in any therapy or marriage counseling prior to divorce.
- Since nearly half of all marriages end in divorce, many children are victims of divorce.
- Parents convicted of abusing drugs often are not required to enroll in rehab programs.
- Up to half of all motor vehicles in some states are operated without insurance coverage. (Guess who pays for the uninsured!)
- Many repeat offenders of drunk driving laws continue driving and are among the drinking drivers who are involved in over one-third of all fatal motor-vehicle accidents. (Guess who is often seriously injured or killed!)
- Minors are allowed to purchase firearms and use them without any supervision by their parents or other responsible adults.
- In most communities, minors are allowed to be out on school nights and weekends without any adult supervision as long as they wish and their parents allow them to do so—or because their parents have no control over them.
- The tobacco industry receives about $40 million annually in support from the government—even though we know that smoking costs the health care system billions annually.
- Smokers are allowed to pollute the air in most indoor facilities that serve the public. The fact that they are often restricted to certain areas usually provides little protection for non-smokers from second-hand smoke. Non-smokers, as a result, are subjected to a serious health hazard against their will and, like smokers, suffer health problems that contribute to health care costs.

— Subsidies are provided for sugar farmers, wool producers, and producers of various other agricultural products.
— Current income tax law is set up to promote the redistribution of wealth.
— Children born in America to mothers who are not American citizens are automatically granted citizenship and all the rights, privileges, and benefits that are included with it—just as are children born to mothers who are citizens. This has resulted in thousands of expectant mothers from less affluent countries entering America temporarily each year, legally and illegally, for the sole purpose of giving birth to their children in America.
— Individuals who enter this country illegally are entitled to some of the same benefits and services that citizens are entitled to. This has contributed to hundreds of thousands of individuals from less affluent countries entering this country illegally each year and has severely strained facilities and funds for citizens, especially in Florida and in states bordering Mexico.

DIRECTIONS FOR RESPONSIBLE CHANGE

The following questions, arguments, and recommendations provide new directions for society and government. As will become apparent, the questions focus on three themes: *individual responsibility, family and parenting*, and *responsible government*. Each question addresses a current policy or condition that allows or encourages individuals to behave in a destructive or irresponsible manner. Judged by the policies currently in place, the questions are moot. But laws, policies, and programs can be changed. Some of the following proposals may appear to be rather drastic and raise constitutional questions and questions about universal human rights. But we are faced with conditions that threaten the very fabric of society. Bold, fundamental changes are needed.

The overall effort must necessarily include both *preventive* and *punitive* measures, with the emphasis on prevention. Why more emphasis on prevention? Because it is the right thing to do. As a compassionate, democratic society, we have an obligation to establish conditions that promote the development of individuals who are assets to their families, communities, and nation. It also makes sense because it is more cost effective than doing nothing until the individual is "in trouble with the law." Preventive measures, then, will result in fewer wasted lives and fewer victims of crime, and will eventually reduce expenditures on fighting crime. The punitive effort, unfortu-

The Challenge of the New Millennium

nately, will have to consist of beefed up efforts and expenditures to fight crime since so many individuals are already involved in criminal activities. Why? Society has an obligation to protect its members from those who lead destructive, anti-social lives and prey on innocents. These efforts should result in stiffer enforcement of current and proposed laws *and* increased efforts to intervene early on to prevent recurrence of destructive behaviors. The goal is to promote the development of *responsible* individuals who care for and respect each other's rights and property. When necessary, this will mean *forcing* individuals to be responsible for themselves and to be considerate of others, and, when preventive and rehabilitative efforts fail, their separation from society.

The effort must rest on three pillars: *education, early intervention,* and *protection of the general public.*

Education should focus on helping children develop values, morals, knowledge, and skills that will lead to socially-constructive lives. It must include compensatory programs, such as Head Start, for children from disadvantaged backgrounds. It should also include a parent education program that is designed to help parents set up home environments that promote healthy child development, and a job training program (and child care) for adults who lack marketable skills. Education and rehab programs should also be provided for those convicted of various crimes. How much will this cost? Billions. But the costs to society will be greater if we do nothing. We either pay for preventive programs now, or we pay more later in blood as well as money. The fact that there are more young African American men in prison than there are in college is reason enough to redouble preventive efforts.

Early intervention should begin with the implementation of programs for children, such as stimulating day care and Head Start. It should also include implementation of parenting programs that begin during pregnancy. Early intervention should also include counseling and therapy for families where marital difficulties, child abuse, or child neglect are apparent. Education, counseling, and therapy programs for those serious offenders who will be returned to society should also be provided.

Protection of the general public should separate from society violent offenders who, despite early counseling and rehab efforts, continue to be a threat to society. It should also provide measures to protect the general public from repeat offenders who pose a serious threat, such as drunk drivers and users of illegal drugs. And it should deal effectively with those who violate common responsibility laws, such as maintaining insurance on motor vehicles and providing court-ordered child support.

Like those changes proposed in Chapters IV and V, then, the following proposals are offered as a way of preventing problems, reducing the recurrence of problems, and protecting the public. They are also offered in the hope that they will result in less crime and enable current recipients of assistance to become more responsible for their own lives and the lives of their children.

The following recommendations are based on the assumption that they cannot all be immediately applied to all *existing* situations. For example, current aid to mothers with dependent children will likely need to be continued, at least on a limited basis, simply because to terminate aid would likely pose a real threat to the well-being of existing children. Rather, what is being proposed is to implement changes at some future date so individuals will be fully aware of the consequences of their behavior *before* they find themselves in a given needy situation. The proposal to limit AFDC to one child, then, would apply only to those who had no children or had only one child when the requirement went into effect. This would also be the case of the proposal to require recipients of public assistance to be high school graduates. Other proposed changes, such as requiring parents to attend parenting classes, should be implemented immediately.

Does this mean more "big brotherism?" On the contrary, the suggestions should result in *less* government interference. They should more effectively enable children and adults to become self-reliant, independent citizens who do not need assistance (and government interference). They should also result in individuals who are more willing to accept the basic responsibilities of citizenship.

Funding for Law Enforcement

Should society provide adequate funding for its courts, law enforcement agencies, and prisons? More to the point: Should society, because of overcrowded prisons, release onto itself those who have been repeatedly convicted of violent crimes? Now these are really absurd questions. But this *is* what is happening. The media report regularly about individuals with histories of violent crimes who commit additional crimes while on probation or after early release and parole. This is outrageous.

Taxpayers are going to have to "bite the bullet." They must provide more funds for courts and law enforcement agencies, and either build adequate prison space or significantly expand the list of crimes punishable by the death penalty. Since society doesn't seem inclined to expand the death penalty, there is but one option—build enough prisons to house those convicted of violent crimes and keep them there.

Tax Reform

Should one of the functions of government be the redistribution of wealth? Enactment of the 16th Amendment in 1913 set the stage for today's progressive federal income tax. It authorized a tax on income—and was first implemented at a one percent rate, with restrictions. But as the need for funds grew, and as social concerns moved to the forefront, it became more *progressive*. Income brackets were established, with progressively higher tax rates as one moved from the bottom bracket to the top. The greater one's income, the greater the tax bite. The basic argument was: Those who earn more can afford to pay more. This progressive income tax marked a fundamental change in thinking in regard to the purpose of the federal government: that it was the duty of government to intervene in the social welfare of citizens by redistributing wealth via a progressive tax system. Did the writers of the Constitution believe one of the functions of government was the redistribution of wealth through taxation? Apparently not since they did not include it. It is also contrary to a fundamental element of capitalism: As an incentive to work, the individual is free to accumulate his own property (wealth) in accordance with his ingenuity, ambition, and willingness to work. He is rewarded, then, according to his efforts.

A *progressive* income tax, which we now have, does just the opposite. Individuals who pursue a better life through education, job training, and careers, and who demonstrate initiative and responsibility in their work are, in effect, punished for their success. They have to give up more since they earn more as a result of their aspirations and willingness to work for a better life. Conversely, those who drop out of school, engage in self-destructive behaviors, and subsequently have low incomes are rewarded for doing so with lower tax rates, even tax credits. This is *fair*? Following this line of logic, it would be fair, for example, to charge the millionaire $100 for a gallon of milk, while the individual with a $20,000 income paid only $2 simply "because the millionaire can afford it." Prices of consumer items, then, would be determined by each purchaser's ability to pay. Those with little or no income could just walk into the local grocery and pick up whatever they wanted free of charge—while those who could pay would make up the difference with overcharges. (Public hospitals are already doing this.)

President Clinton tried to capitalize on this warped sense of fairness when he campaigned against the "rich" in 1994 as if they were a criminal class that didn't pay their fair share. But this was nothing new. Democrats have been saying this for years despite statistics to the contrary. The truth is, as pointed out by the Tax Foundation in Washington, DC, the top 1% of taxpayers, by income, paid nearly 30% of all federal taxes in 1993. The bottom half of taxpayers paid only 5%. So who's paying their fair share?

What would be fair? The progressive income tax should be replaced by either a *flat income tax* or a *consumption tax*. A *flat income tax* would set a specific rate for all taxpayers, regardless of income. Allowing for major elimination of deductibles, the rate necessary for funding federal spending could be in the 15% to 18% range. A 15% rate with no deductibles, for example, would result in the individual with a taxable income of $250,000 paying $37,500 in taxes, and an individual with a taxable income of $40,000 paying $6,000. Those with higher income, then, *would* pay more. What's unfair about this? Absolutely nothing. Taxpayers, regardless of income, would pay a proportional amount in taxes because they would be subject to the same tax rate. What about those with low income? A basic tax-free allowance on income and selected deductibles would ease the burden on those proportionally—yet maintain the element of fairness for all.

What are the chances of adoption of a flat tax? They are getting better. But to secure passage, supporters of a flat tax might have to accept some deductibles and a "cap" on the basic rate, such as 35% on income above $400,000. Such a cap would still allow a generous reward for those with exceptionally high incomes, such as movie stars, professional athletes, lawyers, and CEOs who earn millions annually in royalties, salaries, fees, and stock options. Whatever the case, any cap, like those deductibles/allowables below, should be tied to the rate of inflation. Otherwise, more and more would eventually find themselves in this 35% bracket.

What deductibles and allowances should be retained or included? We need to retain or include the following:

1. A tax-free allowance of $28,000 income per family, or $14,000 per individual taxpayer. Income from non-salary sources, such as royalties, capital gains, dividends, stock options, and interest, would be classified as ordinary income and be subject to the basic tax rate once their total exceeded the allowance described below.
2. A tax-free allowance of $7,500 per year from interest earned on savings and from capital gains and dividends. Why? Americans save much less income than individuals in nearly all other advanced countries. More savings would have three important benefits. First, it would enhance the personal security of families. More funds would be available for emergencies and for various future-enhancement efforts, such as college educations. It would also provide a larger reservoir of funds for financing the national debt—and thereby reduce our dependence on foreign interests. This reservoir would also provide more funds that are essential to economic growth. More funds at lower interest rates would be available for loans to businesses to expand. And expansion means jobs.
3. Mandatory contribution of $2,000 or 5% of income (whichever is less) each year for each taxpayer in a tax-deferred private retirement plan. This should enable individuals to be better prepared for old age.
4. A tax-free deduction of up to $2,000 per year for contributions to approved charities. (With the shrinking role of the government in the welfare of citizens, private organizations will have to carry a bigger load.)
5. A mortgage deduction of up to $14,000 annually. Why? People *have* to live somewhere. Why not in their own home? This deduction would make it possible for more Americans to achieve one of their most cherished dreams—home ownership. There is another benefit: As a major industry, housing creates millions of jobs.

Incorporation of these deductibles/allowances could result in families with incomes up to $55,500 paying *no* taxes.

This change to a flat tax would simplify the preparation of tax returns and reduce the costs of doing so. The maze of rules about deductions, write-offs, and rates that usually require costly professional assistance would be largely eliminated. It would also simplify the task of the IRS and reduce the funds needed for its operations. The only real losers would be those who have a vested interest in maintaining the complicated, ever-changing tax code—those in the business of preparing tax returns, those who represent clients in legal battles with the IRS, and those in the IRS who would lose their jobs because of staff reductions.

A *consumption tax* would be similar to a sales tax. It would require the consumer to pay a tax on any item or service purchased at the retail level. The rate would be the same for everyone. Taxes would be paid as items were purchased—largely eliminating the need for today's bloated IRS. Those who consumed more would pay more. Expenditures for health care and food should be exempted from such a tax, and limited, tax-free allowances for clothing and other basic necessities would be reasonable. What about those in low income brackets? Exemptions for health care and food, and limited, tax-free allowances for clothing and other basic necessities should help those proportionally. Private charities should provide any needed additional assistance.

Whatever the case, we can agree that one of the major problems with the current federal income tax is its constantly changing nature. Members of Congress just can't resist tinkering with tax laws for the benefit some of their constituents—with the hope of enhancing their chances of re-election. This annual tinkering with tax laws should stop. Legislation changing the federal income tax to a flat tax or a consumption tax should also require a two-thirds majority vote in Congress for future changes.

What about *property taxes*? Currently, they provide much of the tax base for funds needed to operate local municipalities and services, such as schools, hospitals, and fire departments. But is it fair to expect only property owners to provide the funds for these needs? No. Funds needed for operation of local public institutions and services should be provided by *all* the local citizenry. Dependence on a property tax allows those who do not own property to enjoy the benefits of local institutions and services without contributing their fair share. The property tax, then, places an unfair burden on those who have been able to accumulate wealth and choose to invest it in real estate. Yes, those who choose to rent rather than own do pay some property taxes since landlords include them in their costs and pass them on to their renters. And those who purchase items in a business are also helping the business owner pay his property taxes since he includes them in his pricing costs. Still, those who do not own real property or choose, instead, to invest most of their savings in non-real estate properties, such as CDs, stocks, and bonds, avoid contributing their fair share. It's time that they do. Property taxes should be abolished. Funds for operation of local public institutions and services should be provided by a flat income tax and/or a consumption tax at the state level. There would be another benefit that most would appreciate. Such a change would eliminate hassles with local appraisal boards.

Subsidies for Producers of Products That Serve No Constructive Purpose

Should financial assistance of any kind (tax breaks, subsidies) be provided to producers of products that serve no constructive purpose and, at the same time, contribute to or cause serious health and social problems? The answer seems obvious. Tobacco products and alcoholic beverages are the most visible examples that fall into this category. Although wine provides limited nutritional benefits (which can easily be found elsewhere), alcoholic beverages provide no major health benefits. On the contrary, their abuse costs society dearly. Alcohol use is often a contributing factor in the emergence of anti-social behaviors, including domestic violence and a wide range of other criminal behaviors. It is also a contributing factor in various diseases, the break up of thousands of marriages each year, and job losses. Even worse, drunk drivers cause or are a contributing factor in one-third of all fatal motor vehicle accidents—over 15,000 fatalities each year. How long would we continue to fight a war that resulted in 15,000 casualties each year?[15] Not long. A massive end-the-war movement would quickly develop. Why, then, are drunk drivers allowed to continue killing thousands each year?

Smoking also costs America dearly.[16] It has been linked to under-developed newborns, weakening of the immune system, diseases such as lung cancer, heart disease, and emphysema, and deaths running in the hundreds of thousands annually. But smoking doesn't just affect those who smoke. It also affects millions who don't smoke because they often must breathe second-hand smoke at work and in facilities that serve the public. What does smoking cost? It adds

---

[15] Actually 17,699 in 1992. From "Traffic Safety Facts" distributed by the National Safety Council. Data compiled by the National Center for Statistics and Analysis, Research and Development; Washington, D.C.

[16] "The U.S. Congress Office of Technology Assessment estimates that cigarettes cost Americans $68 billion annually in tobacco-related health care costs and lost productivity." From *Cancer Facts & Figures 1994*, American Cancer Society, p.22, 1994.

billions each year in health care costs—which could be better spent elsewhere.

What needs to be done? We need to stop kidding ourselves. Nicotine *is* an addictive, destructive drug, and it should be classified as such. Tax breaks should be eliminated immediately, and laws to protect the public from drunk drivers and second-hand smoke need to be strengthened and enforced.

Unlicensed & Uninsured Drivers

Should unlicensed drivers and uninsured drivers be allowed to continue victimizing others? Maintenance of insurance on motor vehicles and demonstration of one's ability to operate a vehicle in a safe, competent manner through a licensing program are basic responsibilities of drivers. Requiring such is both reasonable and prudent. But more and more drivers are shirking these responsibilities. And more and more of us are victims of unlicensed and uninsured drivers every day—and not just in accidents. We have to pay higher insurance premiums, in part, because we feel compelled to include coverage for "uninsured motorist." We are, in reality, being responsible for those who are not. It's time this stopped. For protection of the driving public, the following should be enacted:

— An uninsured motorist will be fined, be required to show proof of insurance, and complete (at his expense) an appropriate counseling/education program on first offense. On second offense during a five year period that began with his first offense, he will be fined, and his motor vehicle will be impounded and his driver's license will be suspended until he shows proof of insurance. On any subsequent offense during that period, his vehicle will be confiscated. Auto insurance companies will be required to report immediately cancellation or non-renewal of policies to appropriate state motor vehicle departments to facilitate compliance.

— A motorist driving without a valid drivers license will be fined on first offense and his motor vehicle will be impounded until he has received his drivers license. On any subsequent offense during a ten year period, his vehicle will be confiscated.

Eligibility for Medicare & Social Security Benefits

Should Medicare and Social Security benefits be available to all citizens, including those who can provide for themselves, or should they be a "safety net"—available only to those who are "in need," that is, those who are unable to adequately provide for themselves? If social assistance is viewed only as a "safety net," Social Security benefits should be available only to those who are "in need." Those who support this position argue that, as a safety net, the benefits are potentially available to every newborn. Upon reaching the designated age, anyone who is unable to provide basic needs for himself would receive assistance. If he did not need assistance, he would not receive it. Supporters argue that this position is similar to a term life insurance policy. It builds no cash value, but it will provide assistance should someone be financially unable to provide for himself. They point out that everyone would have the reassurance that assistance will be available in the event that it is needed.

Those opposed to the above position argue that such an approach is inherently unfair. They ask: If all workers are required to contribute to a fund, is it right to deny benefits to those who managed their personal finances responsibly and accumulated significant assets of their own? If so, middle and upper class members of society will not qualify for Medicare and Social Security benefits—at least until they have depleted their own assets. They are, in effect, punished for managing their lives in a responsible manner. This would conflict with a basic belief of many in society: If individuals are *required* to contribute to a fund, they expect to get something back. Supporters of this position argue that Medicare and Social Security should be like a whole life insurance policy. As policyholders pay premiums, they build cash value and have a right to claim that cash value, including accrued interest.

What are we to do? If Medicare and Social Security continue as currently operated, they face certain bankruptcy. If they are changed to "safety net" programs that provide assistance only to those who are "in need," the threat of bankruptcy will be eliminated. As presently operated, many who do not need assistance receive assistance. And the higher the income group, the more assistance they receive—especially through Medicare. Even worse, under current rules, wealthy recipients often eventually receive assistance that exceeds the total of their contributions and accumulated interest. This is nothing more than welfare for the wealthy. For them, Social Security checks are just "play money." This is unreasonable—and we can't afford it.

What would be fair? Medicare and Social Security should be operated on an "as needed" basis. Assistance, then, would be available to anyone unable to provide for himself. If Medicare and Social

Security are not changed to "as needed" programs, we should at least stop the excessive payments to those who are not "in need." That is, benefits to those who are able to provide for themselves should be stopped as soon as the total reaches the amount that they contributed, including interest. After that, they should provide for their own needs from their own resources.

Agricultural Subsidies

Should producers of agricultural products, especially corporate and wealthy individual producers, receive subsidies (guaranteed price supports)? Subsidies were initially justified on the basis that farm income was substantially lower than that of other occupations with comparable investments. This is a valid point. It was further argued that, since all citizens are dependent on agricultural products, society is, in effect, subsidizing itself. Everyone benefits from plentiful food at cheaper prices. But this isn't necessarily the case. Prices on dairy products, for example, are higher because of "price supports" (subsidies) paid to dairy farmers. (The dairy industry, as a result, lobbied heavily for free lunch in our schools and various dairy products as part of the commodities program for the poor.) Subsidies have also resulted in overproduction and huge, costly surpluses of some products.

Representatives of agricultural interests further argue today that American farm income must be subsidized because of cheap foreign competition. They assert that American farmers cannot compete with foreign farmers because of higher production costs in America, and point, for example, to the much lower cost of rice production in Thailand than in America. They assert that if American farmers do not receive subsidies (price supports), their standard of living will plummet, farmers will go out of business, and America will become dependent on foreign agricultural production. This is the same argument of Japanese rice farmers who demanded that high tariffs on imported rice be maintained. Opponents of subsidies, however, point to the high cost of rice to Japanese consumers as an example of what tariffs and subsidies actually do.

If we really practice free-market enterprise, subsidies must go. Should all subsidies be discontinued? Probably not. We need to conduct a comprehensive, critical examination of all subsidies and eliminate those on most products (and services), significantly reduce those on most others, and end certain practices. Reforms should include a cap on funds that a farmer is allowed, and eliminate the practice of allowing farmers to "rent" their allotment to other farmers. They should end subsidies to individuals who have two occupations, one agricultural and one nonagricultural, and whose agricultural income is less than half their total income that exceeds $100,000. Reforms should also eliminate all support for tobacco farmers.

Assistance to Families with Dependent Children

Should assistance to families with dependent children be continued? This is an issue that stirs strong emotions. Some advocate total, immediate elimination of all assistance. They argue that assistance simply encourages young women to have children so they can qualify for and receive assistance, and that many increase their income by deliberately have child after child. They point to highly publicized "welfare queens" and cases where women with numerous children receive thousands of dollars of assistance each month. But are these cases really the norm? No, they make up a small percentage of the total number receiving AFDC. Few women desire to have child after child simply as a means of income. Most limit their childbearing, and most receive assistance for a short period. And most wish they could be gainfully employed and independent, not dependent on assistance from others.

The problem is, most of those who qualify for AFDC find themselves in need of assistance because of divorce or abandonment and nonsupport of children, self-destructive behaviors such as addictions, job loss, or "stupid" mistakes—unintended pregnancies that occurred during passionate moments. Some teenage girls, however, do elect to have children for a variety of reasons—sometimes as an attempt to "trap" a desirable boy, sometimes just to have something that will "love" them. And some do have children (and additional children) in order to qualify for assistance. Whatever the case, there will continue to be children born into situations where their parents cannot provide even minimum necessities for them. What are we to do?

The first priority should be on forcing the father to be responsible for his child. If he cannot be identified or is unable to provide assistance, the mother's parents or the father's parents should be required to provide for the child. After all, the child is *their* grandchild, not mine, yours, or society's. The first priority, then, should be on encouraging or, if necessary, compelling the family to take care of its own children.

Only after all such avenues have been exhausted should society assume the role of provider. In such cases, a thorough screening process should be implemented following the initial application, including interviews and home visits to verify accuracy of information on the application and the need for assistance. This process should also focus on identifying fraudulent cases, including "double dippers."

Assistance programs should place a considerable burden on the recipient so that being on assistance is not viewed as an attractive lifestyle. To qualify for assistance, then, the applicant must:

1. Begin a program of birth control (using a method such as the Norplant device) to prevent additional births while on assistance.
2. Get a job (public or private) within 16 weeks after assistance begins and work at least 20 hours per week. Child care will be provided during work, but costs of child care will be deducted from earnings.
3. Begin appropriate job training/education programs. School dropouts must re-enroll in school and perform satisfactorily in school. Those who are high school graduates must enroll in a post-high school educational program that may be financed with a student loan.
4. Enroll in and perform satisfactorily in a parent education program.
5. In cases of drug abuse, the recipient must participate in a publicly funded substance abuse program that is designed to cure the problem.

Limitation of Childbearing of Those on Assistance

Does anyone have the right to have an unlimited number of children that society has to provide for because s/he cannot? Current law protects the right of a woman or couple to have as many children as they want—even when society has to feed, clothe, and provide shelter for them. It is defended on the grounds that having children is a universal human right and a matter of personal privacy into which no one can intrude. To do otherwise, then, would be regarded by many as an outrageous intrusion into personal privacy. But should anyone have the *right* to continue burdening society (us) with children they cannot provide for? I think not. Millions do without what they cannot *afford* every day. And for many, this includes children. We delay having children or forgo additional children because we cannot afford them. For us, it's just a matter of being responsible and living within our means. And what's wrong with this? Absolutely nothing.

The Challenge of the New Millennium

We believe that children deserve parents who can provide for their basic needs. If a woman or a couple cannot afford to have children, they should delay having children. If they cannot afford to have more children, they should not have more children.

Unfortunately, individuals and couples who cannot provide for children, do have children. And *more* children. And they expect *us* to feed, clothe, and provide other necessities for *their* children. They believe that we owe it to them. And they are right. Under current law, it is their right—and our obligation. So we provide assistance for child after child. And therein lies the source of considerable resentment and anger: Responsible couples who delay having children or forgo additional children in order to live within their means are *forced* to provide assistance for more and more children of others who do not limit their childbearing in a similar manner. Why the anger? They resent being *forced* to provide assistance to those who do not make similar personal sacrifices.

It's time to deal with this in a responsible manner. If someone is dependent upon public assistance, society should have the right to set limits or restrictions on the behavior (having more children in this case) that creates or contributes to the need for the assistance in the first place. It seems reasonable to require those on AFDC to prevent births of additional children. Enactment of the following requirement would be appropriate:

— To qualify for AFDC, a mother who gives birth to her first child must employ birth control measures (e.g., Norplant) so she cannot have additional children while on AFDC. She will not be provided assistance for additional children. Existing single mothers or couples who already have two or more children and are on assistance must use birth control to prevent additional births. No assistance will be provided beyond that already being received. (If a parent refuses to comply and her children are subjected to serious neglect and deprivation, it will be considered *willful* neglect and grounds for: (1) placement of children in a foster home until the parent becomes able to provide for them or complies with AFDC requirements, and (2) in cases where the parent continues to be unable to provide for her child and refuses to comply with requirements for assistance, putting the child up for adoption after a period of two years in a foster home.)

Unfortunately, this does not solve the problem of those who have children, then, because of an unanticipated event such as job loss or divorce and non-support of children, find themselves in need, unable to provide basic essentials for their children. In cases of divorce, the first effort should be to require the non-custodial parent to provide court-ordered support. Collection should be put on a "fast track." Unemployment benefits should provide temporary assistance for those who find themselves without work.

Mandatory Parent Training

Should parents be required to enroll in parenting classes? Requiring such training could be considered to be an intrusion into the privacy of parents and the family. But since raising a child is one of the most (if not *the* most) complex and important life tasks, and since parenting is more difficult today, it seems that parents need all the help they can get. Indeed, the prevalence of divorced and single parent families, the limited time working parents have to parent, the greater likelihood that children will be exposed to undesirable values and lifestyles, and the temptations and threats to children from violence and drugs present a challenge as never before. And judging from the surge in violent crimes committed by today's teens, many parents are falling short. Parenting classes would surely be very helpful to today's parents—and should be required. Not requiring parenting classes makes even less sense since we commonly require education and licensing for all kinds of less important capabilities, ranging from operation of motor vehicles to landscaping. (No, I'm not suggesting licensing of parents—just mandatory parent education.) Implementation of the following should be a part of the commitment one makes to parenthood:

— Expectant parents must enroll in and begin attending parenting classes during the second trimester of pregnancy.
— Parents must enroll in and complete parenting classes as children enter each major stage of development. This program will focus on (1) establishing a home environment that promotes the child's healthy emotional, social, and intellectual development, (2) establishing a positive relationship with the school, (3) providing good nutrition, (4) dealing with common concerns such as sibling rivalry, sexual maturation, peer pressure, drug abuse, and aggression, and (5) dealing with conflict between parents, between siblings, and between parent and child.
— Parents must attend family counseling and parent counseling sessions when school officials, physicians, or courts believe and

request such as appropriate means of dealing with family problems affecting the child.
— Ongoing parent support groups are available as part of an expanded school program.
— As part of an expanded role of public schools, quality child care shall be available to working parents and parents in educational programs.

Mandatory Work & Job Training For Those on Assistance

Should able-bodied individuals be allowed to receive welfare without working or receiving job training? This was a troubling question to some of those who developed assistance policies in the 1930s. A handout, that is, financial assistance without reciprocal work, seemed contrary to the strong work ethic embedded in society. It still seems reasonable to expect recipients to be available for work. The reality today is that many already on assistance lack marketable job skills and work habits. And there is another factor that must be addressed: Many are single mothers whose children will need child care if they are working. While requiring recipients to work is a reasonable expectation, then, other factors must be taken into account. If the ultimate goal is to get them off assistance, society should facilitate development of job skills where needed, and require recipients to fulfill reasonable work requirements.

Responsible Management of Assistance Programs

Should assistance programs be managed and supervised in a manner that facilitates accomplishment of desired purposes? This is an absurd question. Of course they should. But current administration and supervision of large programs often falls short. Fraud and waste, as a result, are widespread. This is especially the case with Supplemental Security Income (SSI). As noted earlier, SSI currently provides assistance upwards of $400 per month to the disabled. This includes payments to, among others, alcoholics, drug addicts, and disabled children. Assistance checks to alcoholics and drug addicts are often wasted on more booze and drugs—instead of drug rehabilitation and basic necessities. And more and more parents are fraudulently getting their children classified as disabled to qualify for assistance payments. How so? They tell their children to misbehave in school so they can be classified as behaviorally disabled. Others instruct their children to fail a hearing or eye exam so they can be classified as disabled.

What should be done? We need to critically review programs that are riddled with fraud and abuse. SSI is a good example. SSI benefits might be restricted, for example, to those who do not have self-induced disabilities. Or assistance to addicts might cover only the costs of participation in a rehabilitation program and provide commodities during a limited time period. Whatever the case, lawmakers should incorporate into any new assistance program a strict supervisory regimen and adequate supervisory personnel, and make sure that the regimen is reviewed at regular intervals. Unfortunately, Congress does not have a very good record of overseeing programs. Stories of waste and mismanagement are invariably broken by investigative reports—not by those in charge of programs. In cases where investigation verifies initial reports, those who have been negligent in their duties should be fired—not, as often happens in federal agencies, just reassigned. Recipients who have fraudulently received funds should be prosecuted.

Purchase/Use of Firearms by Minors

Should minors be allowed to purchase or use firearms? In view of the number of firearms accidents and shootings by minors each year, it seems reasonable to prohibit the purchase of firearms by minors. Furthermore, if a minor is to use a firearm, he should first receive proper training in the safe use of the firearm. Enactment of the following seems sensible.

— Prohibit minors (under 21 years of age) from purchasing firearms.
— Require minors who wish to use firearms to be trained in the safe and proper use of a firearm before using one.

Mandatory Background Check of Those Who Purchase Firearms

Should individuals be allowed to purchase firearms without a prior check of records for mental illness or felony criminal offenses? This is really an absurd question. Who among us thinks it would be reasonable to place a firearm in the hands of an individual who has a criminal record or a record of serious mental illness? A short delay in the purchase of a firearm for the purpose of checking such records seems reasonable. But don't individuals already have to fill out a form indicating any previous convictions or mental problems? In most states they do. But who's checking to see if their responses are truthful? And what individual with a criminal record or record of mental illness who wishes to purchase a firearm is going to reveal this on a form that he knows won't be checked out? Inclusion of the waiting period in the crime bill in 1994 made sense. In this computer age, it would be easy to check out such records quickly.

Restriction of Smokers & Drinking Drivers

Does anyone have the right to subject anyone else to a serious health risk against their will? Of course not. This has been repeatedly demonstrated, for example, in efforts to remove asbestos materials from schools, to remove various carcinogens from food and water supplies, and in the public anger when it was revealed that citizens were unknowingly exposed to radiation in experiments during the Cold War. What about drinking drivers and smokers? As noted earlier, traffic safety research indicates drinking drivers continue to kill thousands each year. And, as also noted earlier, alcohol abuse is also a contributing factor in tens of thousands of cases of spouse abuse, child abuse, child neglect, and various other crimes each year, and loss of countless days on the job and billions in health care. Other research has recently indicated that secondhand tobacco smoke is a serious health risk to non-smokers. Why do we continue to allow those who smoke and those who abuse alcohol to subject others to serious health risks?

But what about drinkers' and smokers' complaints about their rights? Yes, those who so choose, have the right to smoke and the right to consume alcoholic beverages. But those rights should end when they pose an unacceptable risk to others. We restrict how individuals operate their motor vehicles for the same reason. (If *my* eating of fatty foods contributed to *their* development of heart disease, you can bet that smokers would see the logic in restricting *my* eating of fatty foods.) It's time to protect the public from these risks, as well as drinking drivers from themselves. Does this mean, as some advocate, outlawing smoking and consumption of alcoholic beverages? Of course not. Prohibition was a failure in the 1920s, and it would be a failure today because tobacco and alcohol use continue to be a part of the social fabric in mainstream America. Besides, enacting such would be another example of a growing tendency of the federal government to decide what is good for us. We simply need to protect those who don't smoke from those who do, and to protect ourselves from those who are a threat because of alcohol abuse. Smokers and consumers of alcoholic beverages should be responsible, that is, considerate of others. Implementation of the following should reduce the severity of several problems.

— A driver who is determined to be legally intoxicated by use of alcohol will be fined and required to complete an appropriate education/treatment program on first offense. On second offense, his motor vehicle will be impounded until he completes an appropriate education/treatment program. On any subsequent offense during a ten year period, beginning with his first conviction, his vehicle will be confiscated and he will be incarcerated for a period of one year. (Penalties for offenses which result in fatalities should be harsher.)
— A driver who is in possession of or impaired by use of an illegal drug will be fined and his vehicle will be impounded until he has completed an appropriate education/treatment program. On any subsequent offense, his vehicle will be confiscated.
— An individual who is convicted of any other type of offense, such as domestic violence, in which alcohol is determined to be a contributing factor must complete an educational/treatment program in alcohol abuse.
— Require all indoor work areas and facilities that serve the public to be smoke-free environments, and prohibit smoking at all outdoor public gathering areas such as parks, sport arenas, and other recreational centers.
— Parents who habitually use illegal drugs, become intoxicated by alcoholic beverages, or smoke in their children's presence may be charged with child abuse. Those convicted of such abuses will be required to complete an appropriate education/treatment program.

These laws should be reinforced with the following:

— Prohibition of all advertising of alcohol and tobacco products.
— Implementation of a program in elementary and middle schools designed to educate and prevent children from using illegal drugs, smoking, and consuming alcoholic beverages.

Curfews for Adolescents

Should students in elementary and secondary schools be allowed to be out at all hours of the night without any responsible adult supervision? It's probably in their best interest to be home by a reasonable hour, especially on school nights. (Since when did being home at a reasonable hour ruin any teen?) Yes, teens need to learn how to be independent, responsible citizens. But there's a better time than at two in the morning. Curfews seem reasonable. And, since teens commit a significant number of crimes and are often victims of crime at night, added benefits will be less crime and fewer victims. Preferably, these should be determined by responsible parents, not mandated by government.

School Dropouts

Should students be allowed to drop out of high school? Considering the fact that dropouts are much more likely to end up on public assistance or in prison than those who complete high school, it seems imperative that they stay in school. Indeed, dropping out of school with the 21st century staring us in the face is a personal tragedy that is hard to overstate. Students need to stay in school now more than ever. (For all practical purposes, post-high school education/training is also a must for those who expect to lead a reasonably comfortable life.) It seems reasonable, then, to enact the following:

— Beginning at a specified future date, dropping out of school will be prohibited.

This law will be reinforced with the following:

— Dropping out of high school will result in an indefinite suspension of drivers license, impoundment of one's motor vehicle(s), and ineligibility for public assistance. These requirements will not apply to those who dropped out prior to the specified date of enactment.
— All new mentally able recipients of public assistance must be high school graduates. (General Equivalency Diploma [GED] is unacceptable.)

Mandatory Saving for Old Age

Do people lack self-discipline to the point that government has to force them to save for their old age? Apparently many do. Many are more concerned with today's pleasures than with saving for tomorrow and old age. They behave, in effect, as if they will never grow old. Then they expect others to "help" because of inadequate savings when they can no longer work. Elected officials, always mindful of their political base, then play the compassion/guilt card to persuade the public to be responsible for them. With prudent planning and living, however, most would never need public assistance. The implication is that Social Security retirement benefits should be continued.

Unfortunately, it is widely known that Social Security benefits are not enough.

How can personal savings for old age be increased? Each worker should be required to participate in an individual savings/investment account. Rather than contributing to a general fund as in Social Security, then, each individual should have his own account and accumulate his own assets. Funds should be withheld from his paycheck and deposited directly into his account. The annual contribution should be substantial, such as $4,000 or 7% of gross income, whichever is less. Whatever the case, legislation should make the individual's account untouchable regarding early withdrawals. Access should be limited to conservative investment decisions, such as treasury notes, bonds, CDs, and a limited percentage in stock mutual funds and/or individual stocks. Legislation should prohibit employers and government from using the funds for *any* purpose.

Does this mean more government control? More government encroachment on the freedom of the individual to decide how he will manage his own life? For those who lack the foresight and self-discipline to put aside substantial funds for old age, yes. For those who plan and live prudently, with one eye on retirement, it will have little or no real effect. What it will do, then, is force irresponsible individuals to put aside funds for retirement while still working. In doing so, they will reduce their chances of being a financial burden on others during their senior years.

Tax-Supported College Education

Should the Federal Government provide two years of college education for all who want it? During the 1996 presidential election, one candidate asserted that the federal government should implement an assistance program that would provide two years of college education for everyone who wanted it. This proposal was enthusiastically received on college campuses and by parents across America. After all, who wouldn't want two years of college education for their child—free?

Such a program sounds good. Today's youth certainly need all the education they can get. But whose responsibility is this? Those who support such a notion argue that it would merely be an extension of our tax-supported public schools, that it is logical also to provide two years of college education for all who want it. Opponents, while recognizing the need for post-high school education, assert that it should be the responsibility of parents—not the public. They point out that parents have about 18 years after a child's birth to save for its post-high school education—and that millions of parents have met this responsibility in the past, sacrificing as necessary. Opponents further argue that parents have an obligation to limit family size according to what they can afford—including the cost of post-high school education of children.

I agree. This notion is even more ill-advised in light of the availability of student loans, scholarships, grants and part-time jobs for college students. Such an extension would also be another example of the federal government's assumption of responsibilities that belong to individuals—and another assistance program that would cost billions. And, like countless entitlements before, once enacted there would eventually be efforts to expand it to a four-year college education. Why not even a graduate degree?

The problem is: How would America pay the billions for *another* entitlement? We know there's no such thing as a free lunch—and there's no such thing as a free college education. Somebody has to pay. How would such a program be financed? Despite some promised cuts elsewhere, most likely through more taxes and more deficit spending. Taxpayers of today and tomorrow would be forced to assume an even greater financial burden. (We each already owe about $23,000 as our share of the official six trillion dollar federal debt. [The real debt is considerably higher.]) The question is: How can we seriously consider assumption of such a financial commitment to higher education when we can't even cover current commitments? Public schools in many areas are inadequately funded, many high school graduates are poorly educated, and the federal government is already running large annual deficits. This proposal, then, is ill-advised for several reasons. First, it is a misplaced priority. Public schools need to be attended to first so students can be assured of a first-class education and a diploma that really means something. But it is equally wrong because it would allow parents to shirk a major parental responsibility and increase the number of us who are dependent on government assistance. It would also likely increase the burden on taxpayers and worsen the financial problems confronting America. Furthermore, it would inevitably diminish the quality of a college education. How so? It would result in many high school graduates enrolling in college who shouldn't be there in the first place. College students, under greater pressure to maintain the minimum grade point average required for assistance, would in turn pressure their professors for good grades. And professors, already keenly aware of the threat of lawsuits and how their students' ratings of them affect promotions, tenure and salary increases, would feel more compelled to ease up on their students. The upshot would be more grade inflation. Course requirements would be further watered down so students could get the grades they wanted. Good grades and degrees would be seriously compromised.

Assistance & Benefits for Illegal Aliens

Should America continue to provide assistance and benefits to those who enter America illegally? This is a controversial question, one that evokes strong emotions. Advocates of cutting assistance and benefits to non-citizens point out that providing such benefits has severely strained assistance programs and facilities in some states to the point that our own citizens are being adversely affected. They point to California as a good example, where schools are overcrowded, funds budgeted for public health care have been overwhelmed, and the state is running a large deficit—to a considerable extent because of assistance to illegal aliens. Advocates of cutting assistance to illegal aliens ask, "If such individuals enter illegally in the first place, why should we be required to provide benefits for them?" They believe that providing assistance and benefits acts as a magnet to individuals from less affluent countries, and assert that many will take advantage of benefits as long as they are available. Restricting assistance and benefits to those who are citizens is logical and necessary in their view. They believe nations have an obligation to protect the rights and welfare of their citizens and assert that this includes controlling borders and denying illegal entrees benefits that are supposed to take care of citizens. They argue that those who wish for a better life as American citizens should do so according to the established *legal* process. A more fundamental question in their view is: Should America control its borders? Control of borders, they believe, is not only an important element in providing assistance and services for citizens, but also a key component in the wars against drugs and international terrorism.

Opponents of cuts assert that it is a matter of rights. They argue that cutting assistance and benefits is a violation of universal human rights and argue that denial of benefits to illegal entrees, as in Proposition 187 in California, is not only inhumane and unconstitutional—but also immoral. They claim that most illegal entrees in America are workers who are contributing to the economic prosperity of America. They do not enter America just to get free benefits or assistance, but are looking for jobs and hope to eventually become American citizens.

The problem is implementing such restrictions. Aside from moral considerations, how would we stop children who are illegal entrees from attending public schools? Things could get ugly at the school door. We could end up with hundreds of thousands of uneducated, angry children with little hope out on the streets—which clearly would not be in our best interest. And, should a woman who is an illegal entree about to deliver a baby be denied entry to a hospital because she cannot pay for needed services? Few would be willing to physically block her entry. One possible solution would be to bill the government of the country where she is a citizen. Whatever the case, court decisions will make these questions moot if they decide that such restrictions are unconstitutional.

Since the federal government has failed miserably in its responsibility to control our borders, Americans are now confronted with unpleasant choices. Are all illegal aliens to be "rounded up" and deported? Is it realistic to believe this is possible? If this isn't possible, do we want large numbers of children who are illegal entrees to be left uneducated? We may be stuck with educating those already in the United States. Two things are certain: First, some of the benefits to illegal aliens, such as SSI, should end since they act as a magnet for those from less affluent countries. And second, the Border Patrol should be enlarged by a substantial margin and the process for deporting future illegal entrees should be streamlined.

Citizenship for Newborns

Should we continue to grant citizenship to children born here to mothers who are visitors from other countries or to mothers who enter the United States illegally? Current law automatically grants citizenship to any child born in the United States—regardless of its mother's (or parents') citizenship status. This includes children born to mothers who are not citizens, even those who have entered the country illegally. Such children are granted all the rights, privileges, and benefits that are granted to children born to mothers who *are* citizens. This, of course, serves as a magnet to expectant mothers from less affluent countries. Each year thousands arrive just in time to give birth to their children. Currently, for example, two out of every three babies delivered in Los Angeles County hospitals are born to mothers who are illegal entrees! Yet another example was provided by a neighbor who was a postal worker in Las Cruces, New

Mexico. She told me about a woman who, upon arrival at the post office, became irate because she had to wait for her mail to be put in her box. She was in a hurry to pick up her welfare check (AFDC) and return to her home—in Ciudad Juarez, Mexico. A constitutional amendment is needed to deal with this problem. It might read as follows:

— Citizenship is automatically granted to a child born in the United States whose mother is a citizen of the United States. It is also granted to a child born to a mother who is a legal entree who has been a resident for at least one year and who becomes or is in the process of becoming a citizen of the United States. Citizenship is also granted to a child born to a mother who is an illegal entree when its mother becomes a citizen of the United States. However, a child born to a mother who is an illegal entree shall not, except for education and inoculations provided by public schools, be eligible for benefits or assistance until it becomes a citizen.

Concluding Thoughts

It should be remembered that the above suggestions address only some of the more popular concerns today. Other issues also need to be addressed. Whatever the case, we need to strive for solutions that promote individual responsibility and achievement and the fiscal soundness of America. This means guarding against politicians who make generous campaign promises that, if enacted, would erode individual responsibility, expand government control over citizens, and add to the national debt. It should be remembered that politicians have long recognized the appeal of the "free lunch" and, as a result, typically include them in their quest for votes. Such "feel good" proposals offer financial assistance that, on the surface, will cost recipients (the more the better) nothing. Little is said about their impact on the national debt or who will pay for them. Unfortunately, many voters consider only "what's in it for me." Voters need to take a broader view and judge proposed "free lunches" for what they are and how they will impact the nation as a whole. They need to remember that such proposals, aside from any well-intentioned goals, are attempts by politicians to secure, maintain, or expand their power—and vote accordingly on such issues and support political reforms. Otherwise we make our task more difficult and increase the chances of an Orwellian future.

We also need to promote our common heritage as a society. Why? Historically, large diverse societies that have withstood the test of time have been based on individual achievement and common strands that bind various groups into a greater whole. If we are to endure as a society, then, fairness requires that we promote certain basic universals—which include, among other things, families that instill common desirable moral values in their children, courts and law enforcement agencies that promote equal justice, a political system that promotes fair representation in government, reasonable opportunities for individuals to achieve economic success, effective education in public schools, and a common language. Otherwise self-serving, destructive forces of *the beast within* will play a greater role in the behaviors of individuals and in government. We will continue to grow as a nation of dependents, and the balkanization of America will continue. America will be increasingly divided along racial and ethnic lines with growing strains on the union, or an eventual break-up as in the Soviet Union. Should this occur, we will all lose.

About the Author

The author's higher education includes a Bachelor of Science, a Master of Education, and a Doctor of Education—which include studies in various social sciences. As an undergraduate at Sam Houston State Teacher's College, Dr. Hicks completed a major in history and minors in sociology and economics. During studies for a master's degree at Sam Houston State College and for a doctorate at the University of Northern Colorado, he completed numerous advanced courses in history, psychology, sociology, anthropology, and education.

Upon completion of his bachelor's degree, Dr. Hicks began service as a social studies teacher in a public middle school. He later returned to college to begin advanced studies, culminating in a master's degree in 1968 and a doctorate in 1970. He taught at the college level until returning to public schools in 1983. His service as a classroom teacher in the mid-1960s, then in the mid-1980s, provided opportunities for first-hand observations about changes and problems in children, families, and society in general.

Dr. Hicks' early personal background provided part of the impetus for this work. With experiences as a youth in a small town in the "Fifties" serving as a baseline, he, like others, has observed significant changes in American society—changes that seemed to take on a more destructive nature in the 1980s and 1990s. These changes and his concern for our future as a society prompted him to produce this work. It is based on countless experiences and observations as a teacher, as a student of human nature, and as a concerned citizen. He offers sensible answers to problems in our families, in schools, and in society as a whole.

Dr. Hicks has written about various problems in education and in society. His most recent work, *Let's Get Serious About Teaching Children to Write*, was published by University Press of America, Inc. in 1993.

INDEX

A

Abuse
  Child 34, 96, 115, 133, 159, 175
  Physical 115
  Sexual 115
Addiction 30, 142, 156, 166, 169, 173
Adrenaline 29, 34, 50
Aesthetics 39, 43
AFDC (see Aid to Families With Dependent Children)
Affective Domain, core of 56
Aggression 23-24, 43
Agricultural Adjustment Administration 137
Aid to Families With Dependent Children (AFDC) 135, 140, 148, 155, 160, 171, 182
AIDS 18, 25, 93
Alcoholic beverages 74, 77, 99, 165, 175-176
Alcoholism 97, 100, 114, 133, 142, 156, 165, 173
Aliens, Illegal 135, 142, 180-181
Altruism 54
Amendments
  To bills 136
  To U.S. Constitution 137, 146, 153, 154, 161, 182
American Civil Responsibilities Association (ACRA) 145
Anger 34, 39, 42, 65, 108, 171
Asbestos 175
Assassinations 41

B

Baird, Zoe 85
Balanced Budget Amendment 146, 155

Barnum, P.T. 84
Beast Within, The 14-20
Behavior 51, 57
  Altruistic 54
  Paradoxical 60-61
  Violent 49
Behavioral Modes 42
Behavioral Standards 49
Big Bang 38
Bird watching 50
Border Patrol 135, 142, 181
Boxing 23, 30, 50
Branch Davidians 33
Bullfighting 23, 30, 50
Bungee jumping 30, 67

C

Campfires 36
Camping 51, 78, 114
Caring 35, 44, 91, 96, 115
Charities 163
Chess 50
Children 99
  Raising 101
  Setting limits on 115
Citizenship 52, 117, 121, 158, 160, 176, 181
  For Newborns 181-182
Civil Rights Movement 64, 86, 125
Civilian Conservation Corps (CCC) 137
Clergy 18
Clinton, William 146, 147, 162
Cockfighting 50
Code, Internalization of 46
Cold War 13, 64, 175
Coliseum, Roman 23
College 74, 100, 105
  Community 80

Financing 111, 142, 163
Community
  Functions of 48-49
  Sense of 11, 93, 115
  Status 21, 44
Compassion 17, 35, 42, 44, 63, 130, 138, 149, 177
Compatibility, Social 51-55
Competition 24-25
Connell, Richard 50
Conscientious objectors 64
Constitution, U.S. 64, 146, 153-155, 158, 161, 182
Contraception 70, 75, 89, 132, 170, 171
Contract for America 147
Control, Social 69-72
Council for Government Reform 146
Counseling
  Family 76, 132, 159, 172
  Marriage 97, 133, 157
Crime 11, 13, 41, 46, 58, 75, 93, 94, 133
  Capital 161
  In schools 92
  Kidnapping 157
  Murder 89
  Prevention 135, 158
  Sexual assault 89
  Teenage 70
  Violent 88, 92, 108, 160
Crusades 27, 41
Curfews 73, 79, 176

D
Dark Side, The 15
Darwin 24
Debt, National 86
Declaration of Independence (American) 64

Depression, Great (1930s) 137-138
Differences
  Between 1950s & 1990s 68, 86
  Human 41, 48-51
  Philosophical 151
  Settling 17, 40, 91
  Values 56, 61, 80
Discipline 121
Disease 165
  Heart 175
  Sexually transmitted 18
Divorce 22, 28, 34, 88, 114, 144, 157, 172
  Children of 76, 92, 95, 100, 132
  Control of 71
  Coping with 132, 133, 157
  Rate of 77, 80, 91
Dress codes 121
Drugs 99
  Abuse 93, 97, 100, 133, 142, 156, 172, 173
  Illegal 75

E
Education
  Bilingual 141
  College 178
  Parenting 144
  Sex 106
Emotions 34-35

F
Fairness 28
Family 32-34, 95
  Breakup 18
  Counseling 76, 132
  Functions of 48-49
  Gay/Lesbian 34
  Mother-Child 34

Family Counseling 159, 172
Farm Credit Administration 137
Fear 11, 30, 34, 38, 46, 67, 70, 133
Federal Deposit Insurance Corporation (FDIC) 137
Federal Housing Administration (FHA) 137
Feelings Log 128
Firearms 157, 174-175
Fireplaces 36
Fishing 51, 78
Football 23, 30, 50
Formative Years 53
Freedom 144

G
Gambling 30
Games
  Chess 50
  Danger and escape 30
  Football 50
  Hockey 50
  Video 30
Gandhi, Mahatma 28
General Equivalency Diploma (GED) 133, 177
Germany, Nazi 41
Great, Society, The 138
Guilt 177

H
Hang gliding 67
Hate 13, 23, 27, 34, 35
Health care 139
Hiking 51
Hockey 30, 50
Holy Land 27
Hoover, Herbert C. 137
Hunters
  Deer 31
  Illegal 50
  Social 31
Hunting 20, 26, 30-32, 50, 51, 78, 97

I
Identity (as individuals) 21, 95, 97, 132
Immigration & Naturalization Service (INS) 142
Incas 41
Incest 18
  Emotional 111
Insanity, temporary 42
Instincts 16, 18, 98
  Environment-specific 16-17
  Fight or Flight 29-30, 34, 43
  Nesting 19
  Power 23
  Sex 35, 103
  Survival 53
Insurance
  Bank 137
  Life 89, 167
  Motor Vehicle 90, 135, 157, 160, 166
  Unemployment 135, 138, 148, 172

J
Jealousy 65
Jenkins' Ear, War over 41
Jesus 52
Job Corps 138
Johnson, Lyndon B. 138

K
Kennedy, John F. 24
Kidnapping 157
King, Martin Luther, Jr. 28, 64
Kohlberg, Lawrence 61, 107, 108

L

Language 39-40, 53, 183
   Body 21, 34
   Foreign 141
   Street 80, 99, 101
Lawsuits 91, 127
Learning
   Readiness for 76, 118
   Role of 48
Licenses
   Driving 22, 103, 166, 177
   Motor Vehicle 21
Limbic System 43
Lincoln, Abraham 52
Locomotion, Bipedal 33
Logic, Problem Solving 29
Love 20, 34, 35, 63

M

Mandela, Nelson 28
Marriage 18, 78
   Broken 21
   Commitment 71, 77
   Pregnancy before 70
   Reasons for 34
   Schools and 132
Marriage Counseling 97, 133, 157
Maturity 60
   Children 113
   Cultural 49
   Moral 55, 59, 61-65, 129
   Sexual 33, 35, 81, 96, 172
   Social 40
McGuffey Readers 123
Medicaid 148
Medicare 141, 147, 148, 156, 166-168
Moral Values 58
Morality 54, 55, 56, 92, 122, 123, 125
   Importance of 59-60
Most Dangerous Game, The 50
Movies 19, 24, 30, 50, 72-73
   Sex in 80, 92, 101
   Violence in 89, 101
Murder 58, 89
Music 19, 39, 91, 100

N

National Park Service 135, 142
National Youth Administration 144
Nations, Third World 26
Nazis 41
Neglect, child 34, 96, 115, 133, 159, 171, 175
New Deal 137-138, 139
Nicotine 166
Norplant 170, 171
Nutrition 134, 172

O

Obedience 62-65
Order, Social 25
Orientations
   Good Boy-Nice Girl 62
   Instrumental-Relativist 62
   Law and Order 63
   Punishment-and-Obedience 61
   Social-Contract/Legalistic 63
   Universal-Ethical-Principle 63
Other-Awareness 54

P

Parenting 80, 102-116, 158, 172
Parents
   Single 76, 77, 79, 80, 92, 93, 96, 98, 100, 106, 117, 127, 133, 140, 144, 157, 173
Pecking Order 25, 47
Peer Pressure 172
Photography 50

Play 40
Political Correctness 92
Political parties 25, 131, 147
Politicians 27, 139, 151
Politics 84-86
  Corruption 93
  Power 23, 27, 33, 136, 150-151
Post-Traumatic Stress Disorder (PTSD) 42
Power
  Control 26-28, 59, 107
  Limiting 153
  Politics 23, 27, 33, 136, 150, 151
  Sharing 25
  Status 27
  Structure 26
  Struggles 13, 41, 147
Predators 32, 97
Pregnancy 18, 70, 172
  Unwanted 18, 70
Principles of Survival 118
Priorities 56
Problem solving 43
Prohibition (of alcohol) 175, 176
Punishment 46, 52, 56, 62, 64, 70, 71, 77, 107-109, 113, 123, 161
  Capital 57
  Fear of 52, 108, 136
  For being responsible 167
  Natural disasters as 37
  Values and 58

Q
Quayle, Daniel 92

R
Racing
  Automobile 23
  Horse 30

Radiation 175
Rational thought, displacement of 40
Recreation 30, 67
Reforms 153
  Banking 137
  Fiscal 155, 168
  Political 86, 145-158
  Tax 161-165
  Welfare 136, 140
Reinforcement 52
Relationships 27, 44, 49, 57, 70, 104, 120, 130, 156
  Economic 55
  Extra-marital 18
  Family 61
  Sexual 18, 33, 97
  Social 31, 55
  Symbiotic 138
Reproduction 35-36, 43
Responsibility 80, 90, 97, 110, 115, 118, 120, 134-136, 145, 150, 158, 160
  Agents of 51
  Fiscal 86, 146
Revenge 27, 44
Rewards 26, 49, 52, 109, 126, 154
Rights 45, 49
  Civil 64
  Individual 17, 63, 134, 144
  Of Newborn 104, 132
  Property 21
  Universal 55, 64, 158, 180
  Water 21
Rogers, William Penn Adair (Will) 84
Roller coasters 30
Roman Empire 41
Roosevelt, Franklin D. 137

Rural Electrification
  Administration (REA) 137

S

Sacrifice 35
School dropouts 90, 135, 140, 156, 170, 177
Schools 106, 117-133
  Curriculum 120
  Discipline in 76
  Drug in 117
  Drugs in 75, 76, 80, 176
  During 1950s 69, 70, 73-74, 76, 87-88
  Overcrowding 135
  Problems at 100
  Public 75-77, 81, 108, 122, 134, 137
  Purposes of 119-120
  Security at 75, 90, 117
  Segregated 86
  Sex in 75
  Teaching values in 94, 123, 125, 126-131
  Values 118, 120-127
  Violence at 89, 92, 117
Sects, religious 33
Self-esteem 22, 95, 110, 133
Service, Community 53, 145
Sex 32, 70, 75, 80, 105
  Abstinence 70, 132
  Appeal 18
  Drive 18-20, 35, 81, 96, 103
  Intimacy 70
  Premarital 70, 88, 89, 91
Sexual assault 89
Single Parents 76, 77, 79, 80, 92, 93, 96, 98, 100, 106, 117, 127, 133, 140, 144, 157, 173
Sky diving 30
Soccer 23

Social Security 138, 141, 146, 148-150, 154, 156, 166-168, 177
Speech 43, 54
  Freedom of 131, 150
  Holophrastic 40
  Telegraphic 40
Spiritualism 36-39
Sports
  Aggressive 23
  Spectator 23
SSI (see Supplemental Security Income)
Status
  Community 21, 44, 71
  Power 27
Steinbeck, John E. 138
Stock Market, Crash of 1929 22
Subsidies 165, 167
  Agricultural 138, 141, 148, 158, 168-169
  Tobacco 85, 157
Suicide 22
  Teenage 99, 122
Supplemental Security Income (SSI) 140, 142, 156, 173, 181
Survival of the Fittest 24
Symbiosis 138

T

Tax Foundation 162
Taxes 85, 122, 132, 143, 149, 161-165
  Fear and 62, 108
  Income 137, 158, 161
  Luxury 137
  Property 136, 164
Teacher Corps 142
Television 78
  Sex in 80, 101
  Violence in 101

Territorialism 20-22, 43
Three-Brain Concept 43
Tobacco 77, 85, 90, 165, 169, 175, 176
Trauma 95, 110
Tutu, Bishop 28
Twain, Mark (Samuel Langhorne Clemens) 129

U

Unemployment 133, 135, 138

V

Vacations 78
Values 56, 80, 123, 125
  Family 95
Video games 30, 100
Violence
  Boxing 50
  Bullfighting 50
  Cockfighting 50
  Crime 13, 41
  Football 50
  Wresting 50
Voting 131

W

War 41
  Civil 137
  Cold 13, 64
  Desert Storm 27, 41
  Protests 125
  Vietnam 125
  World War II 27
Weapons 26
  Biological 13, 26
  Chemical 13
  Conventional 26
  Nuclear 13, 26
  Research 61
Welfare 74, 90, 136, 138, 139-143, 156, 163, 173, 177
  AFDC 135, 140, 148, 155, 160, 171, 182
  Dependence on 90, 106, 139
  Illegal Aliens 180
  Medicaid 148
  Social 161
  SSI 140, 142, 156, 173, 181
Welfare Queens 169
World War I 137
World War II 80
Wrestling 50